DAILY WARM-UPS

Grade

Social-Emotional Reflections

Author
Samantha Chagollan

Editor
Sara Connolly

Editor in Chief
Brent L. Fox, M. Ed.

Creative Director
Sarah M. Fournier

Cover Artist
Diem Pascarella

Art Coordinator
Renée Mc Elwee

Illustrator
Crystal–Dawn Keitz

Imaging
Crystal–Dawn Keitz

Publisher
Mary D. Smith, M.S. Ed.

Teacher Created Resources
12621 Western Avenue
Garden Grove, CA 92841
www.teachercreated.com

ISBN: 978-1-4206-1702-3

©2022 Teacher Created Resources
Reprinted, 2022

Made in U.S.A.

For standards correlations, visit
http://www.teachercreated.com/standards/

Teacher Created Resources

Table of Contents

What Is Social-Emotional Learning?

Social-Emotional Learning (SEL) helps students recognize and understand their emotions, cope with emotional situations, and develop empathy. These skills are crucial to students' development and can help them navigate responsible decision-making for the rest of their lives.

According to the Collaborative for Academic, Social, and Emotional Learning (CASEL), SEL involves five areas of competency:

- ✦ Self-Awareness—knowing your own emotions
- ✦ Social Awareness—understanding others' emotions and dealing with social situations
- ✦ Self-Management—regulating your own emotions
- ✦ Responsible Decision Making—solving problems and having accountability
- ✦ Relationship Skills—establishing relationships and communicating with others

While SEL has become more widely discussed recently, the concept dates back to research that began in the early 1960s. Various studies over the years have found that SEL has proven to help students with:

- ✦ Goal setting and accomplishment
- ✦ Self-assessment and self-control
- ✦ Decreasing physical aggression
- ✦ Improving academic proficiency

When students learn how to cope with their emotions, they are better able to give and receive feedback, bounce back from disappointments, and focus when they need to—all of which can help them excel academically. An emotionally well-adjusted student is a successful student.

Beyond helping students perform better academically, learning social emotional skills early in life can help students thrive throughout their lives. SEL teaches students valuable qualities that will benefit them in their future jobs, academics, and personal pursuits.

Daily Emotional Reflections

Why start the day with SEL? Many successful people start their day with mindfulness: meditation, daily journaling, morning affirmations, etc. That's because centering yourself first thing in the morning gets you focused and ready to tackle whatever your day has in store.

For students, taking a few moments each morning to check in on how they're feeling can start a habit that they can build on for the rest of their lives.

Each of the exercises in this book is designed to help students spend a few moments in the morning to check in with themselves, and to learn a little bit about the spectrum of human emotions.

When your students start their day with emotional awareness, they will be more likely to carry that awareness with them throughout the day, helping them to make good choices and have empathy both inside and outside of your classroom.

 ## How to Use This Book
— The Emotions —

Each of the first sixteen units explores a different emotion, with two activities each devoted to these fundamental aspects of SEL:

✦ **Defining the Emotion**

Explaining what the emotion is; asking students to reflect on what they already know about it

✦ **Identifying the Emotion in Others**

Asking students to think about what the emotion looks like in other people; helping to develop empathy

✦ **Identifying the Emotion in Yourself**

Detecting how the emotion looks and feels in their own experience; developing self-awareness and self-assessment

✦ **Strategies for Dealing with the Emotion**

Exploring different coping strategies for the emotion; helping to develop self-regulation and encouraging healthy social interactions

✦ **Putting It All Together**

Reflecting on what they have discovered about the emotion; exploring what strategies they will try in the future

Note: You don't have to work through this book in order; you can start or end with any emotion.

The final unit, All the Feelings, is intended for students to experience once they have learned about all of the different emotions. This unit gives them a chance to reflect on how the different emotions can complement and conflict with each other, and offers ideas on how to manage a mix of feelings.

— The Emojis —

In today's social world, most students are very familiar with emojis and the feelings they represent. In this book they are presented as a simple, visual way for students to identify with different feelings.

In each unit, there are at least two activities that start with an emoji emotional check-in. This is a great and simple way for students to check in with their own feelings first thing.

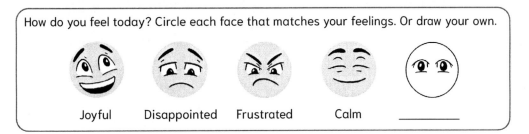

How do you feel today? Circle each face that matches your feelings. Or draw your own.

Joyful   Disappointed   Frustrated   Calm   _____

— Mindful Moments & Yoga Breaks —

Each unit also offers a meditation suggestion and a breakdown of a simple yoga pose that complements the emotion featured in that unit. Breathing and movement exercises could be done individually, or throughout the week by the entire class.

— Fun Facts, Quotes & Tips —

Throughout the book, you will also find fun facts, quotes, and quick tips about the featured emotion of the unit. These can be interesting discussion starters as you segue into the next part of your lesson plan.

Creating a Kind Classroom

A kind and welcoming classroom is an ideal place for students to learn and discover more about their feelings.

It's important that your students feel encouraged to discuss feelings when they come up, and that beyond these morning exercises, your class is a safe place for them to feel all of their emotions.

Here are some other ideas and activities to expand your SEL teachings beyond morning reflections.

✦ Create a Mindfulness or Calm-Down Corner that is a quiet space for students to reflect; a few pillows and a yoga mat can create a welcoming place for breathing or journaling.

✦ Watch the movie *Inside Out* as a class, and invite a discussion afterward about the emotions featured in the film.

✦ Incorporate yoga and/or breathing and meditation as part of your daily or weekly lessons, maybe creating regular events like Meditation Monday or Yoga Friday.

✦ Model good emotional behavior—talk about how you're feeling, and point out the feelings and emotions of characters in stories featured in your class.

✦ Play a feelings game such as Emotional Charades, in which students are given an emotion to act out for others.

✦ Create a classroom poster of coping activities that students can choose from when their emotions are distracting them from focusing.

✦ Have the class make a collage of positive affirmations that can be referred to throughout the year as needed.

✦ Encourage and reward random acts of kindness both inside and outside of the classroom.

> "There's no 'should' or 'should not' when it comes to having feelings. They're part of who we are and their origins are beyond our control. When we can believe that, we may find it easier to make constructive choices about what to do with those feelings."
> –Fred Rogers

Name: _____   **Date:** _____

What does it mean to feel afraid?

When we are scared of what might happen next, we say, **"I feel afraid."**

What color would you choose for fear? Color in the circle with that color. Then, draw a picture about feeling scared using only that color.

Fear is just a feeling, like happiness, sadness, or anger. Once you understand what scares you, you can learn how to deal with it. That doesn't mean you will never be afraid again! But you might feel a little less afraid.

Name: _____ Date: _____

I feel afraid! I also feel...

Here are some other words for feeling afraid:

Scared   Frightened   Spooked

When you feel afraid, you might also feel:

Nervous   Worried   Upset

Draw a picture of the last time you were afraid. What were you afraid of?

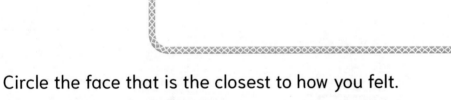

Circle the face that is the closest to how you felt.

What makes you feel less afraid? _____

_____

Name: _____ **Date:** _____

Can you tell when someone is afraid? Their eyes might get big. They might yell or scream! Or they might be very quiet.

When someone is afraid, what does their voice sound like? _____

_____

_____

What does their face look like? Draw a picture of someone who is scared.

How do they act? What do they do with their body? _____

_____

_____

Yoga Break

If you're feeling scared, try Child's Pose. Begin on your knees. Sit back on your heels. Bring your forehead to the ground. Stretch your arms out in front of you. Take three deep breaths.

Name: _____ Date: _____

Frightful Friends

You might be afraid of big dogs. But your friend might be afraid of little dogs.

You never know what is behind someone else's fear!

Let's partner up. Ask your partner which choice below they would be more scared of. Circle their answer. Then use a different color and circle your answers.

What's Scarier?		
Spiders	OR	Snakes
Bad dreams	OR	Scary movies
Thunderstorms	OR	Fireworks
Sharks	OR	Clowns

Are any of your answers the same? _____

_____

_____

> If someone tells you they are afraid of something you think is silly, please don't make fun or laugh! Their fear is very real to them. The best thing you can do is be a good friend and help them feel better.

Name: _____   **Date:** _____

That's scary!

When you're scared, it can be a big or a small feeling.

Sometimes feeling scared feels like a jolt. Like when somebody jumps out and surprises you.

Sometimes feeling scared makes you tense up. Like when you know the scary part of the story is coming.

Let's look at what makes you feel afraid.

What is one thing that scares you? _____

_____

_____

What makes it scary? _____

_____

_____

Draw a picture of what you do when you are afraid.

Do you ever like feeling scared? Sometimes we even *enjoy* feeling scared, like when we tell each other spooky stories. Fear can be kind of fun sometimes!

Name: _____　　**Date:** _____

How do you feel today? Circle each face that matches your feelings. Or draw your own.

　　Tired　　　　Brave　　　　Happy　　　　Shy　　　　_____

How do you know when you're feeling afraid?

Think about the last time you were feeling scared.

Where did you feel it in your body? Did your heart beat a little faster? Did you tighten up your shoulders?

How does feeling afraid look for you?

When I'm scared, my face looks like this:　　　　When I'm afraid, this is where I feel it in my body:

　　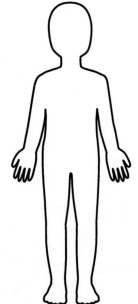

When I feel scared, I might also be feeling...

_____

_____

_____

Name: _____   **Date:** _____

Super Brave

Fear is just a feeling with a job to do. Fear is trying to protect you from getting hurt.

But sometimes feeling afraid stops you from doing something you want to do. You can try being brave instead.

Being brave doesn't mean you're not afraid anymore. You can choose to be brave and still feel afraid too.

Imagine that being brave is your superpower!

Draw a picture of yourself as a brave superhero.

What do you say to yourself when you are feeling brave? _____

_____

What is something you could say to someone who is feeling scared? _____

_____

_____

_____

Name: _____ Date: _____

Have Courage

Having courage is just like feeling brave.

When you have courage, you can deal with being afraid.

Imagine you have all the courage that a lion has.

What is one thing that scares you that you would like to try to be less afraid of?

_____

_____

Name one person you know who has courage. _____

_____

What is one thing you could do to feel better the next time you feel afraid?

_____

_____

Mindful Moment

You can calm down by giving yourself a big hug. Cross your arms in front of your chest. Close your eyes. Take a deep breath in. As you breathe out, squeeze yourself tight. Try this for three long, deep breaths.

Name: _____ **Date:** _____

Write a letter and draw a picture for someone who is afraid. Give them some ideas about how to face their fear.

Here are some things to include:

- Who is the letter for?
- What are they afraid of?
- How do you think they can face their fear?

_____

_____

_____

_____

_____

_____

_____

Name: _____   **Date:** _____

How do you feel today? Circle each face that matches your feelings. Or draw your own.

Silly   Proud   Scared   Calm   _____

Here's what I know now about fear:

When I'm afraid, I feel like… _____

_____

_____

_____

When I'm afraid, I think… _____

_____

_____

_____

Draw a picture of what you will do the next time you feel afraid.

Name: _____   **Date:** _____

What is anger?

Anger is what we feel when things aren't going our way.

When we are feeling mad, we say **"I feel angry."**

What color would you choose for anger? Color in the circle with that color. Then, draw a picture about feeling angry using only that color.

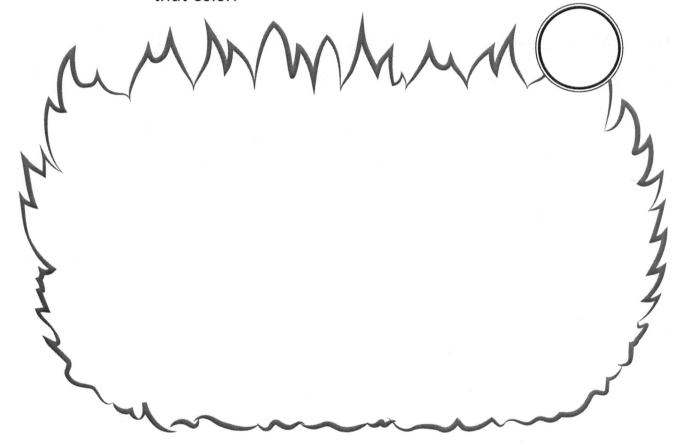

What do you know about feeling angry? _____

_____

_____

We all get angry sometimes! Sometimes we have other feelings at the same time. You might also feel sad or jealous. Talking to someone about how you feel can help.

Name: _____ **Date:** _____

I feel angry! I also feel...

Here are some other words for feeling angry:

Frustrated Mad Furious

When you feel angry, you might also feel:

Confused Hurt Afraid

Draw a picture of the last time you felt angry.

Circle the face that is the closest to how you felt.

Yoga Break

When you're feeling mad, try Downward Facing Dog Pose. Begin on your knees. Place your hands on the floor in front of you. Then lift your knees and straighten your legs. You should be in an upside-down "V" shape. Take a few deep breaths.

Name: _____   **Date:** _____

How do you feel today? Circle each face that matches your feelings. Or draw your own.

Worried   Brave   Angry   Sad   _____

When someone is angry, how do they look?

Some may stomp around and yell.

Others are quiet when they are mad. Or they may stop talking to you.

What do you think an angry person looks like?

When someone is angry, what does their voice sound like? _____

_____

_____

What does their face look like? Draw a picture of someone who is angry.

How do they act? What do they do with their body? _____

_____

_____

Name: _____ **Date:** _____

  # Chill Out

When a problem is hard to solve, it's easy to feel angry.

But it's much easier to solve a problem when you're calm!

When you are calm and chilled out, you are in control. You're the boss—not your anger!

Name someone you know who can stay calm, even when they are mad.

_____

Draw a picture of the calm person you chose.

How can you tell they are calm? _____

_____

_____

Mindful Moment

Taking a deep breath helps when you feel mad. Let's practice! Take a deep breath in through your nose and count to three at the same time. Slowly let the breath out through your nose. Repeat three times or until you feel calm.

Name: _____　**Date:** _____

Mad Monsters

Sometimes when we get angry, we act out. We can say unkind things. Or shut down completely.

It's almost like a Mad Monster steps in and takes control!

Circle the traits that sound like you when you get angry. Then color the Monsters.

CRABBY	GRUMPY	CRANKY
• Throws things	• Gets quiet	• Cries
• Screams	• Pouts	• Runs away
• Hits	• Doesn't want to play anymore	• Wants to be alone

Which Monster shows up most often when you get mad?

_____

Name: _____   **Date:** _____

What's bugging you?

We all have things that bug us and make us angry.

We call these triggers. Your triggers might be different from someone else's.

It helps to know what your triggers are. Then you can spot your anger before it gets out of control.

What are some things that make you feel angry? Color the ones that trigger you.

I don't get what I want.

Someone yells at me.

Things are not fair.

I lose a game.

I get in trouble.

I'm being ignored.

One thing I can say or do to cool down when my triggers show up:

_____

_____

_____

Someone tells me what to do.

Name: _____ **Date:** _____

Hot Like Lava

We all feel angry sometimes. Sometimes we are a little angry, and it's no big deal.

Other times, our anger grows into a bigger feeling. Then it erupts like a volcano!

Choose a color for each section of the volcano. Color in the volcano. Draw a face to match each section.

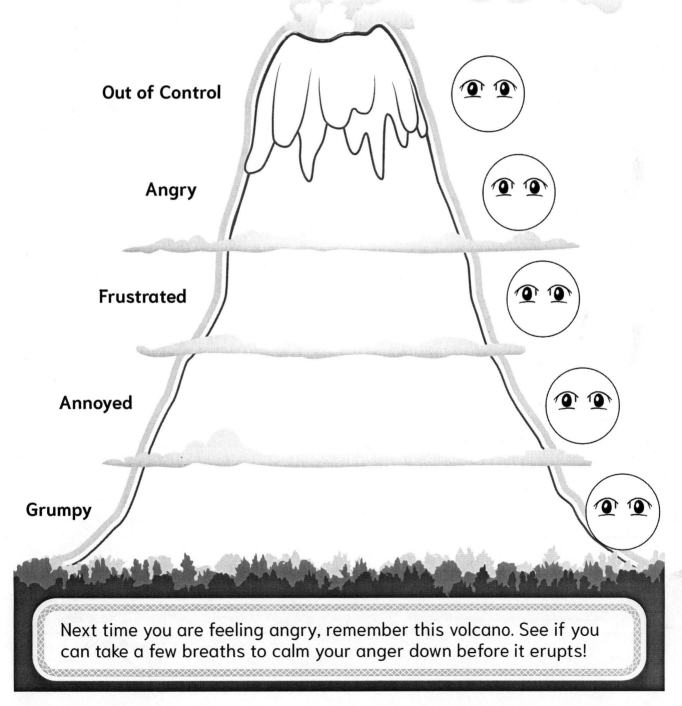

Out of Control

Angry

Frustrated

Annoyed

Grumpy

Next time you are feeling angry, remember this volcano. See if you can take a few breaths to calm your anger down before it erupts!

Name: _____ **Date:** _____

Staying Calm

When something makes you mad, take a breath. Notice: *I'm feeling a little angry right now.*

You can ask yourself, "Why do I feel angry?"

The next thing you can do is calm yourself down. It's okay to be angry. It's not okay to act out.

Here are some ideas on how to calm down. Circle the ones you would try.

What I can do to calm down:

Take a walk outside

Draw or paint

Dance for 5 minutes

Ask a friend to play

Take a break

Take 5 deep breaths

Listen to music

Read a book

Do a yoga pose

Sing a song

What is one new thing you would like to try the next time you feel angry?

_____

_____

Name: _____ **Date:** _____

Your Choice

You can't avoid getting mad sometimes. It's just a part of being human!

But you can learn how to cope with your anger when you feel it.

When you are angry, you have a choice. You can calm yourself down. Or you can act out.

Here are some ways you can act when you are angry. Circle the calm choices in blue. Circle the acting-out choices in red.

Take a deep breath	Count to 5
Ask for help	Ask for a hug
Throw something	Say mean things
Talk it out	Hit someone
Scream	Think about something else

Name: _____   **Date:** _____

How do you feel today? Circle each face that matches your feelings. Or draw your own.

      Down   Excited   Angry   Goofy   _____

Here is what I know now about feeling angry:

When I'm angry, my brain is saying… _____

_____

_____

When I'm angry, I feel… _____

_____

_____

Draw a picture of what you will do the next time you feel angry.

Name: _____   Date: _____

What is anxiety?

Anxiety is what we feel when we aren't sure about what will happen next.

We say, **"I feel anxious."**

What color would you choose for anxiety? Color in the circle with that color. Then, draw a picture about feeling anxious using only that color.

What do you know about feeling anxious? _____

_____

_____

We all feel anxious or worried sometimes. But feeling anxious all the time can stop us from having fun. That's why it's good to notice when you're feeling anxious. Then you can find healthy ways to cope.

Name: _____   **Date:** _____

I feel anxious! I also feel...

Here are some other words for feeling anxious:

Worried   Nervous   Uneasy

When you feel anxious, you might also feel:

Afraid   Embarrassed   Stressed

Anxiety is a little different than fear. You might be **afraid** of the dark.

But you might feel **anxious** when you think about falling asleep without a light tonight.

Anxiety is how your mind and body react to something that *might* happen in the future.

Have you ever felt anxious? Draw a picture about it here.

Circle the face that is the closest to how you felt.

What makes you feel less anxious? _____

_____

Name: _____ **Date:** _____

Feeling anxious can look different in everyone.

Sometimes anxiety feels or looks like fear. Sometimes it's more like a quiet worrying.

What does an anxious person look like?

When someone is anxious, what does their voice sound like? _____

_____

_____

_____

What does their face look like? Draw a picture of someone who is anxious.

How do they act? What do they do with their body? _____

_____

_____

_____

Are you worrying about something? Try to focus on your breath instead. It gives your brain something to do! Is your friend feeling anxious? Try asking them to take some deep breaths with you. It might help them feel less alone or worried. And you might feel better too!

Name: _____ **Date:** _____

Does it worry you?

Find a partner. Read each situation below. Decide if it worries you or not.

A "thumbs up" means yes, it worries you. A "thumbs down" means no, it doesn't worry you.

Record your own rating and your partner's. Then answer the last question on your own.

My Rating	Worried or Not?	My Partner's Rating
👍 👎	There's a thunderstorm coming.	👍 👎
👍 👎	You have to take a test.	👍 👎
👍 👎	You don't have anyone to sit with at lunch.	👍 👎
👍 👎	You have to learn something new.	👍 👎
👍 👎	You didn't get invited to a party.	👍 👎

Now choose one thing your partner said worries them. What would you say to help them feel better?

_____

_____

_____

_____

Name: _____ **Date:** _____

How do you feel today? Circle each face that matches your feelings. Or draw your own.

Proud   Upset   Calm   Friendly   _____

How can you tell if you're feeling anxious? You might feel it in your body.

Sometimes anxiety feels like butterflies in your stomach. You could feel a little shaky. You might feel like your heart is beating a little faster.

How does feeling anxious look for you?

Is there anything you are worried about right now? Explain your answer.

_____

_____

_____

When I feel anxious, my face looks like this:

When I feel anxious, this is where I feel it in my body:

When I feel anxious, I also feel… _____

_____

_____

Name: _____　　Date: _____

Sometimes what we are worried about is out of our control.

For example, you can't control the weather. You can't stop a storm that is on the way. But you can go indoors out of the rain. That is probably in your control.

When you're feeling anxious, it helps to separate the things that are in your control from the things that are not.

Choose items from the list below. Draw a line to show which side they belong to. Add your own ideas too.

My attitude

Homework

Weather

My words

Others' feelings

In My Control　　My thoughts　　**Out of My Control**

Others' actions

What I wear

Time

My effort

My choices

Name: _____   Date: _____

Happy Thoughts

When you're feeling anxious, your mind can get stuck. You keep thinking the same thing. The more you think about it, the more worried you feel.

You might think: "I'll never be any good at this."

But you could think: "If I keep working at it, I can improve."

Draw a line to match each worried thought with a happier thought.

Worried Thoughts

I can't do this.

What if something bad happens?

No one wants to play with me.

I don't know the answer.

Happy Thoughts

I have a lot of people who love me.

I can get help if I need to.

What if something good happens?

I can learn how to do this.

Mindful Moment

Sit or lie down. Close your eyes. Breathe slowly in and out through your nose. Think about your happy thought. Say it to yourself as you take a deep, slow breath in. Say it again as you slowly let your breath out. Repeat five times.

Name: _____   **Date:** _____

Let it go!

If we held onto all of our worries, we would be worried all the time!

You can let go of the things you can't control. You can let go of worried thoughts too.

What are some worries you can let go of?

In the balloons below, write down a few of the thoughts or ideas that you are ready to let go.

Mindful Moment

Choose one of the thoughts or ideas. Close your eyes and take a slow breath in. As you breathe out, imagine you are letting go of that thought. Watch it float like a balloon, up into the sky, until it disappears.

Name: _____   **Date:** _____

How to Get Grounded

Grounding yourself is a way to remind your brain that you are safe and in control.

Using "5–4–3–2–1" is one way to ground yourself. It slows your mind down.

Let's practice it now.

	Name 5 things you can see.	_____ _____ _____ _____ _____
	Name 4 things you can touch.	_____ _____ _____ _____
	Name 3 things you can hear.	_____ _____ _____
	Name 2 things you can smell.	_____ _____
	Name 1 thing you can taste.	_____

Name: _____ **Date:** _____

How do you feel today? Circle each face that matches your feelings. Or draw your own.

Hurt   Happy   Excited   Loved   _____

Here's what I know now about anxiety:

When I am feeling anxious, my brain might be thinking… _____

_____

_____

When I'm anxious, I feel… _____

_____

_____

Draw a picture of what you will do the next time you feel anxious.

Yoga Break

Tree Pose is perfect when you're feeling a little anxious. Stand on one leg. Place your other foot on the inside of the leg you are standing on. Lift your arms up like the branches of a tree. Take three deep breaths. Then repeat on the other side.

Name: _____   Date: _____

What does it mean to feel bored?

What does it mean to feel bored?

When we say, **"I'm bored,"** we're saying that we've run out of ideas. We don't know what to do next.

What color would you choose for boredom? Color in the circle with that color. Then, draw a picture about feeling bored using only that color.

What do you know about feeling bored? _____

_____

_____

_____

It's hard to be bored when you're curious! The next time you are feeling bored, try being curious instead. What colors can you see? Can you name everything you can see? What can you hear?

Name: _____ Date: _____

I feel bored! I also feel...

Here are some other words for feeling bored:

Tired　　　　　Uninterested　　　　　Frustrated

When you feel bored, you might also feel:

Annoyed　　　　　Down　　　　　Irritated

Everyone feels bored sometimes. Sometimes your brain just needs a break!

Think about the last time you felt bored. Draw a picture about it here.

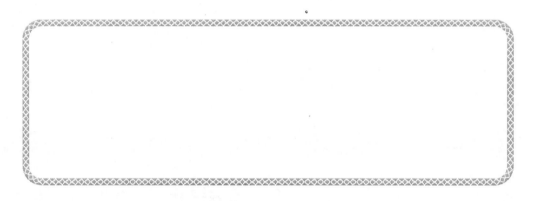

Circle the face that is the closest to how you felt.

What do you usually do when you feel bored? _____

_____

_____

Name: _____ **Date:** _____

How do you know when someone is bored?

Do they get really quiet? Or extra loud and excited?

Everyone shows their feelings differently. Let's try to break it down.

When someone is bored, what does their voice sound like? _____

_____

_____

_____

What does their face look like? Draw a picture of someone who is bored.

How do they act? What do they do with their body? _____

_____

_____

_____

Name: _____　**Date:** _____

How do you feel today? Circle each face that matches your feelings. Or draw your own.

Disappointed　　Brave　　Scared　　Shy　　_____

Boredom Buddies

Find a partner and ask them these questions. Write or draw their answers.

What is the most boring thing you can think of?	
What were you doing the last time you felt bored?	
What is one thing that never bores you?	

Yoga Break

Try this with your partner! You're going to make a double tree. Stand next to each other. Bend your outside leg (the one that is not next to your partner). Turn that knee out to the side. Lift your outside arms straight up towards the sky.

Name: _____ **Date:** _____

What does it look and feel like when you are bored?

When you are feeling bored, you might be feeling sad or frustrated too.

Your brain just wants to take a break from that other feeling. So it tells you that you're bored!

Draw a picture about the last time you were feeling bored. What were you doing?

When I feel bored, my face looks like this:

When I'm bored, this is where I feel it in my body:

When I feel bored, I might also be feeling... _____

_____

_____

Next time you're feeling bored, ask yourself: "How am I really feeling right now?" If you're feeling sad or worried, try drawing about it. It might make you feel better.

Name: _____ **Date:** _____

How do you feel today? Circle each face that matches your feelings. Or draw your own.

Jealous   Silly   Happy   Sad   _____

This is so boring!

What is the most boring game? _____

What is the most boring song? _____

Where is the most boring room at home? _____

What is so boring that it almost puts you to sleep? _____

_____

_____

Draw a picture of one thing that *never* bores you.

Name: _____ **Date:** _____

Bust that boredom!

What are some new things you'd like to try?

Are you feeling bored? That's the perfect time to try a new challenge!

Check off which of these you would try. Write or draw a few of your own too.

☐ Read a book   ☐ Write a story

☐ Make your own game   ☐ Draw your favorite animal

☐ Plant something   ☐ Call a friend

☐ Paint rocks   ☐ Study the stars

☐ Build a fort   ☐ Do a puzzle

☐ Play soccer   ☐ Bake a treat

Some other things I can do when I'm bored:

Name: _____   Date: _____

Dear Me

What would you say to yourself the next time you are bored?

Write a postcard to yourself. Remind yourself of something you could do the next time you feel bored.

Dear _____,
(your name)

Next time you are bored, you should try this:

_____

_____

_____

_____

Draw a picture of an exciting place.

Name: _____ **Date:** _____

Dream Big

Next time you are feeling bored, try daydreaming instead.

You're still awake, but you can let your mind wander. It's time to think about big ideas. You could also think about the future.

Draw or write about your daydreams here.

I like to dream about…

Someday, I want to…

If I could have one wish come true, it would be…

"You may say I'm a dreamer, but I'm not the only one." –John Lennon

Name: _____   **Date:** _____

Here's what I know now about feeling bored.

When I'm bored, my brain is saying... _____

_____

_____

_____

When I'm bored, I feel... _____

_____

_____

_____

Draw a picture
of what you will
do the next time
you feel bored.

Mindful Moment

Feeling bored? Take a brain break! Close your eyes or look down.
Take three long breaths in and out. Then ask yourself, "What do I
want to do right now?" Listen for what your mind says.

Name: _____ **Date:** _____

What does it mean to feel calm?

Calm is a happy, relaxed feeling. When you're feeling peaceful, you can say, **"I feel calm."**

What color would you choose for calm? Color in the circle with that color. Then, draw a picture about feeling calm using only that color.

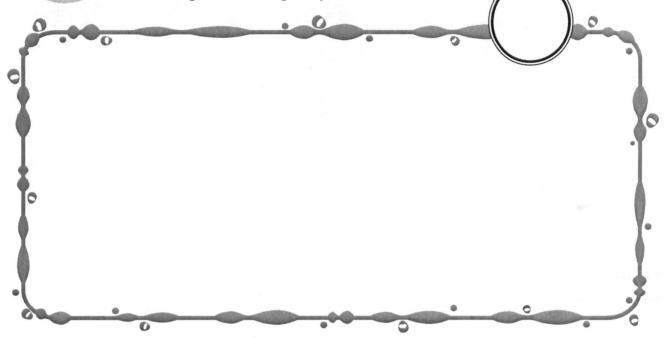

What do you know about feeling calm? _____

_____

_____

_____

Mindful Moment

Belly Breath helps you feel calm. Sit down and close your eyes. Place one hand on your chest and the other on your belly. Try to take a deep breath down into your belly. Feel your belly get bigger with your breath. As you slowly exhale, feel your belly get smaller. Repeat five times.

Name: _____   Date: _____

I feel calm! I also feel...

Here are some other words for feeling calm:

Peaceful   Relaxed

When you feel calm, you might also feel:

Happy   Hopeful   Tired

Calm is a happy feeling. But no one can feel calm all of the time! We have lots of different feelings. But feeling calm can help when we're feeling upset or stressed.

Think about the last time you felt calm. Draw a picture about it here.

Circle the face that is the closest to how you felt.

What helps you feel calm? _____

_____

_____

Name: _____ **Date:** _____

How do you know when someone is feeling calm?

Some calm people are quiet. Others are loud, but they may still be calm!

What do you think calm looks like?

When someone is calm, what does their voice sound like? _____

_____

_____

_____

What does their face look like? Draw a picture of someone who is calm.

How do they act? What do they do with their body? _____

_____

_____

_____

Name: _____　　Date: _____

What feels calm?

Which of these things feel calm?

Circle your answers. Then answer the prompt below.

Trees	A roller-coaster	Fireworks
A concert	Turtles	Mountains
A napping cat	A soccer game	Playing outside
A hammock	The beach	

Name a place, a thing, or a person that always helps you calm down:

_____

_____

Name: _____ **Date:** _____

How do you feel today? Circle each face that matches your feelings. Or draw your own.

Joyful   Disappointed   Frustrated   Calm   _____

Think of a happy memory when you were feeling calm. What were you doing?

_____

_____

When I feel calm, my face looks like this:

When I'm calm, this is where I feel it in my body:

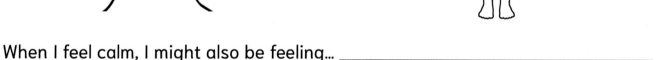

When I feel calm, I might also be feeling… _____

_____

Yoga Break

Airplane Pose can help you feel calm and peaceful. Just like you are flying through the sky! Lay on your belly and stretch your arms out to a "T." Keep your legs straight and lift them off the ground. Lift your head and chest too. Take at least three deep breaths and fly!

Name: _____ Date: _____

Calm Vision

What if you had a special pair of calm glasses?

No matter how mad or sad you are, these glasses are like magic! Every time you put these special glasses on, you instantly feel calm.

Think of a time your calm glasses would have come in handy. What was happening?

_____

_____

What would have been different if you were wearing your calm glasses?

_____

_____

What words describe how you would feel with your calm glasses on? _____

_____

_____

Draw a picture of
yourself with your
calm glasses on.

Name: _____ **Date:** _____

Calling on Calm

Small feelings are small. They come and go quickly.

Big feelings can feel huge! They can even get out of control. A big feeling can even ruin your whole day!

When you have a big feeling, calling on your calm can help make it a little smaller.

Cut out the feelings at the bottom of this page. Choose the ones you think are big and the ones you think are small. Place all the big feelings together. Place all the small feelings together.

Big Feelings	**Small Feelings**

 Scared   Mad   Lonely   Sad

 Hurt   Tired   Shy   Silly

Name: _____　　Date: _____

My Peaceful Place

Imagine the calmest place you can think of. It can be a real place. It can also be a place you made up.

It can be a room, a building, or a city. It's up to you!

Close your eyes and take a few deep breaths. Imagine all the details of this peaceful place.

- What colors are there?
- What does it sound like?

- What does it smell like?
- What does it feel like?

Draw a picture of your peaceful place, and write about it below.

_____

_____

_____

Name: _____ **Date:** _____

In My Calm Bubble

When you're calm, you can listen better. You can pay attention to what is happening.

Imagine that you have a giant bubble around you. Everything inside your bubble helps you stay calm.

Draw yourself in the center of this calm bubble. Then write or draw all the things that help you feel calm. You can add your pet, your favorite music, or a friend who helps you calm down. It's your bubble, so add what you want!

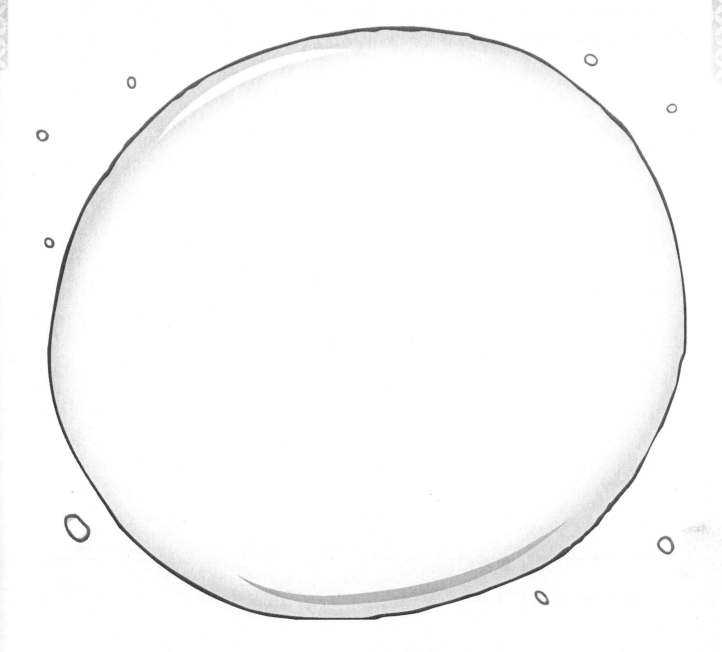

Name: _____   **Date:** _____

How do you feel today? Circle each face that matches your feelings. Or draw your own.

Friendly   Worried   Proud   Tired   _____

Here's what I know now about calm:

When I'm calm, I can... _____

_____

_____

_____

_____

When I need to calm myself down, I can... _____

_____

_____

_____

_____

Next time you are feeling mad or sad, try to remember your calm feeling. It can help you decide what to do next!

Name: _____ Date: _____

Do you know what confidence is?

When you're feeling good about yourself, you say, **"I feel confident."** Feeling confident means you are sure you can do it.

What color would you choose for confidence? Color in the circle with that color. Then, draw a picture about feeling confident using only that color.

What do you know about feeling confident? _____

_____

_____

_____

Yoga Break

When you need a boost of confidence, try Warrior Pose. Step one foot forward. Bend your front knee. Keep your back leg straight. Raise your arms straight up towards the sky. Look up and take three deep breaths.

Name: _____   Date: _____

I feel confident! I also feel...

Here are some other words for feeling confident:

Brave   Proud   Determined

When you feel confident, you might also feel:

Excited   Hopeful   Loved

Confidence is what helps you do big things. When you are confident, you are brave.

When is the last time you felt confident? Draw a picture of what was happening.

Circle the face that is the closest to how you felt.

Why do you think you felt confident? _____

_____

_____

Name: _____ **Date:** _____

How does a confident person look?

Confidence is not the same as bragging. It's more of a quiet feeling inside. But you can tell when someone is feeling confident.

What do you think feeling confident looks like?

When someone is confident, what does their voice sound like? _____

_____

_____

_____

What does their face look like? Draw a picture of someone who is confident.

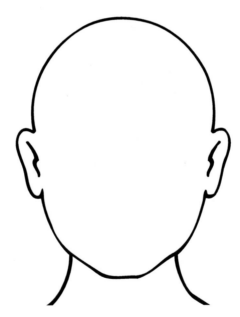

How do they act? What do they do with their body? _____

_____

_____

_____

Name: _____   Date: _____

I'm confident in you!

Confidence is something you can build in yourself. You can help someone else build theirs too, with compliments!

Find a partner. Sit across from each other. Give your partner three compliments. Then they will give you three compliments. Write down the compliments your partner gives you. Write down their name too. Be sure to thank them!

Then write three compliments to yourself. What do you like about you?

Compliments from my partner:

1. _____

2. _____

3. _____

Thanks, _____!

Compliments to myself:

1. _____

2. _____

3. _____

Name: _____ **Date:** _____

When you are feeling confident, you feel like you can do anything.

You believe in yourself. Even if someone else thinks you can't do something, you know you can do it.

How does it look and feel when you are confident?

I feel most confident when I am... _____

_____

_____

_____

When I feel confident, my face looks like this:

When I'm confident, this is where I feel it in my body:

When I feel confident, I might also be feeling... _____

_____

_____

_____

Name: _____ **Date:** _____

How do you feel today? Circle each face that matches your feelings. Or draw your own.

Lonely   Confident   Upset   Happy   _____

Shining Bright

Let's make a list of all of the amazing things about you. Next time you are not feeling very confident, you can read this list and remember!

Draw a picture of yourself in the center. Then write your answers.

I am really good at

_____

_____

_____

One special thing about me is

_____

_____

_____

I am proud of

_____

_____

_____

I am happy when

_____

_____

_____

Name: _____ **Date:** _____

My Goals

How do you get more confidence?

One way is to set a goal for yourself. Then work hard to make it happen!

When you set goals and reach them, you will build your confidence. Then you can reach more goals!

What is one thing you would like to do better?

What are three small steps you can take towards your goal?

Who can help you achieve your goal?

- _____
- _____

Name: _____　**Date:** _____

Mind your thoughts!

Does your brain ever tell you, "I can't do this" or "this is too hard"?

When you think a thought like that, it's easy to believe it's true.

But did you know you can change that thought? You can think a new thought.

You could say to yourself instead, "I can do hard things!" and "I believe in myself!"

Let's practice! For each of these negative thoughts, write your own positive thought instead.

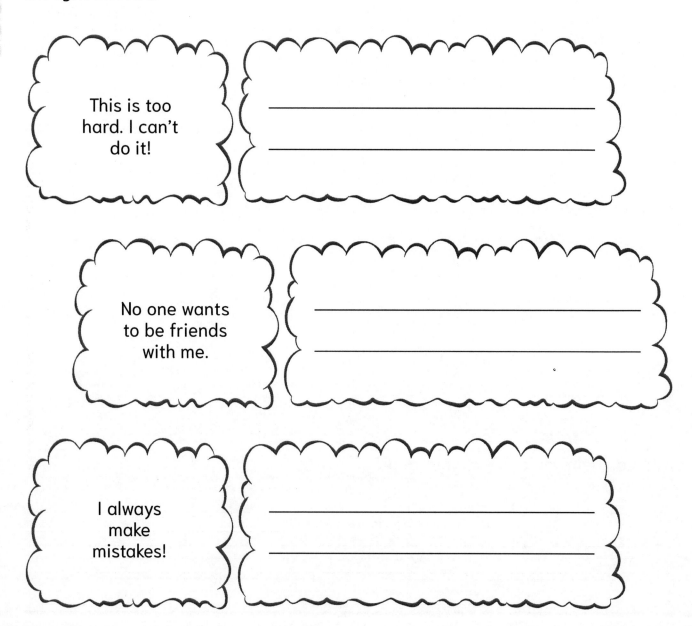

This is too hard. I can't do it!

_____

_____

No one wants to be friends with me.

_____

_____

I always make mistakes!

_____

_____

Name: _____ **Date:** _____

How do you feel today? Circle each face that matches your feelings. Or draw your own.

Calm   Scared   Shy   Embarrassed   _____

The Confidence Suit

What if confidence was something you could wear? Imagine you had a suit that you could put on when you need a little extra confidence.

When you are wearing your Confidence Suit, you don't let any negative thoughts in. You are confident in everything you do and say.

What would that be like?

What does your suit look like? Draw a picture.

Who will you talk to? _____

_____

_____

What will you do? _____

_____

_____

_____

What will you try that you've never tried before? _____

_____

_____

Name: _____   **Date:** _____

Here's what I know now about feeling confident.

When I'm confident, I'm thinking… _____

_____

_____

When I'm confident, I'm feeling… _____

_____

_____

The next time I'm not feeling very confident, I'm going to remember… _____

_____

_____

Draw a picture
of yourself
feeling confident.

Mindful Moment

Start your morning with confidence! When you wake up, sit for a few moments with your eyes closed. Take a few long, deep breaths. Say silently to yourself, "I am confident." Or try one of these sayings: "Today is a good day," or "I believe in myself."

Name: _____ **Date:** _____

What is disappointment?

When things don't turn out the way we hoped, we can feel disappointed. When we were hoping for something else, we say, **"I feel disappointed."**

What color would you choose for disappointment? Color in the circle with that color. Then, draw a picture about feeling disappointed using only that color.

What do you know about feeling disappointed? _____

_____

_____

_____

Disappointment is just a feeling like happiness or anger. Even though it can seem like it will stick around forever, it will go away. We just have to learn how to cope with it while it sticks around!

Name: _____ **Date:** _____

I feel disappointed! I also feel...

Here are some other words for feeling disappointed:

Sad

Discouraged

Defeated

When you feel disappointed, you might also feel:

Worried

Down

Frustrated

When we are disappointed, we may also feel sad or frustrated. If you were hoping to go on a trip with your family this summer, but your plans got canceled, you would feel disappointed.

You might also feel down or discouraged. You might worry that you'll never get to go on a trip again.

When was a time you felt disappointed? _____

_____

_____

Circle the face that is the closest to how you felt.

What do you usually do when you are disappointed? _____

_____

_____

Name: _____ **Date:** _____

Everyone handles disappointment in a different way.

Some people might cry or get very quiet. Others might yell and scream and throw a tantrum.

What does disappointment look like to you?

When someone is disappointed, what does their voice sound like? _____

_____

What does their face look like? Draw a picture of someone who is disappointed.

How do they act? What do they do with their body? _____

_____

_____

How else do you know someone is disappointed? _____

_____

_____

Some people like to be comforted when they are disappointed. But others may want to be alone. If you think someone is feeling disappointed, you can ask them if they want a friend. You could say, "You seem a little down. Do you want to talk about it?"

Name: _____   **Date:** _____

Play Date

Lily is excited to visit the park today. She can't wait to play on the slide!

She walks to the park after school with her best friend. They talk about what games they are going to play. But when they get there, they see a sign. "Park Closed Today," it says. Oh no!

How do you think Lily feels? _____

_____

_____

_____

Why do you think she feels that way? _____

_____

_____

_____

If you were Lily, what would you do? _____

_____

_____

_____

If you were Lily's best friend, what would you to say her? _____

_____

_____

_____

Name: _____ **Date:** _____

How do you feel today? Circle each face that matches your feelings. Or draw your own.

Confident   Friendly   Invisible   Loved   _____

How does disappointment feel for you?

It may feel like a heavy stone in your belly. Or you might feel a little shaky or upset instead.

When was the last time you felt disappointed? Draw a picture about it here.

When I feel disappointed, my face looks like this:

When I feel disappointed, this is where I feel it in my body:

When I feel disappointed, I may also feel... _____

_____

_____

Name: _____ Date: _____

Is it a big deal?

When things don't go how you want, how disappointed are you?

It probably depends on what happened, and what you were hoping for.

Rate how disappointed you would be for each of these situations. Color in the circle that fits you best.

	No Big Deal	Kind of a Big Deal	A Big, Huge Deal
You open up your lunch to find your favorite treat is missing.	◯	◯	◯
When you wake up, it's pouring rain.	◯	◯	◯
You're about to watch a movie— and your friend tells you the ending.	◯	◯	◯
Your favorite shirt has a huge stain on it!	◯	◯	◯

Name: _____   **Date:** _____

Oops! I made some art.

Do you know anyone who has *never* made a mistake?

Everyone makes mistakes!

You might feel disappointed in yourself when you make a mistake. But mistakes help us learn too.

To prove it, we're going to practice making some mistakes. And then we'll make that into art!

Read the directions first, then get to work!

1. Grab a marker or crayon.

2. With your eyes closed, make a squiggly line.

3. Turn this page upside down.

4. With your eyes closed, draw a straight line.

5. Turn the page right–side up again.

What do you see? Turn it into a beautiful piece of art.

(**My Masterpiece**)

Name: _____   **Date:** _____

A Silver Lining

There is a saying: "Every cloud has a silver lining."

It means that even when it's cloudy and raining, there is something good waiting to happen. It's like the rainbow that comes after the rain.

Name one silver lining for each rain cloud. Then color in the rainbow.

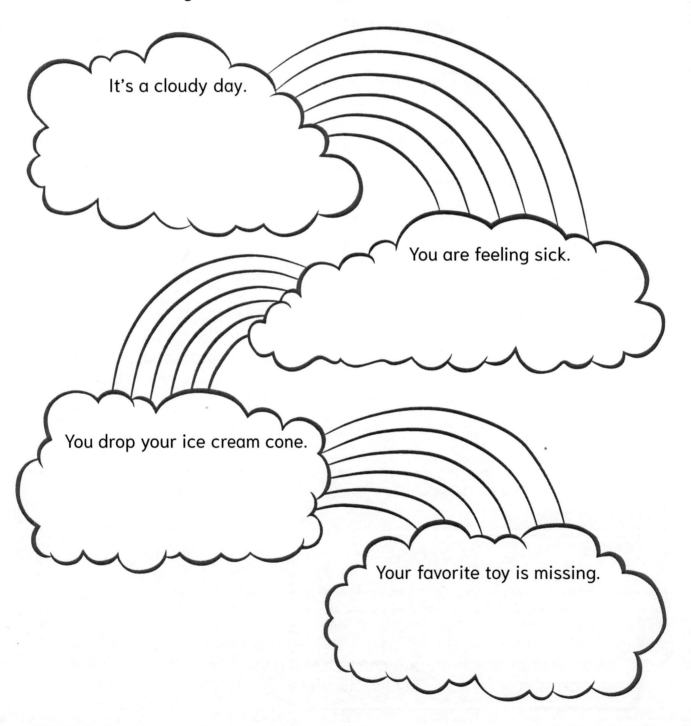

Name: _____ **Date:** _____

Keep Growing

Everyone is disappointed sometimes. What counts is how you deal with disappointment.

Do you keep going? Do you keep growing?

You already have what you need to keep going! Write what you have in the flowers below. Add color if you want!

When I'm disappointed, I can keep growing.

Who helps me
feel better:

What I can
say to myself:

A happy song
I can dance to:

A story or game
that can help:

One thing that will
make me feel better:

Yoga Break

If you're feeling a little disappointed, Knees-to-Chest Pose can help. Lie on your back. Bend both knees. Bring them into your chest. Wrap your arms around your shins and give yourself a hug.

Name: _____　**Date:** _____

How do you feel today? Circle each face that matches your feelings. Or draw your own.

Creative　　　Hopeful　　　Calm　　　Left Out　　　_____

Here's what I know now about disappointment:

When I'm disappointed, I feel... _____

_____

Next time I feel disappointed, I will try... _____

_____

_____

Draw a picture of something you are grateful for. Remember this the next time you're feeling disappointed.

Mindful Moment

It's hard to feel disappointed when you are grateful. To focus on feeling grateful, try this. Place one hand on your heart and one hand on your belly. Close your eyes. Take a few deep breaths. Think of three things you are grateful for. When you're ready, take one last deep breath. Then open your eyes.

Name: _____   **Date:** _____

What is disgust?

When you say **"I feel disgusted,"** you're saying you don't like something. You can feel disgusted by something you smell, taste, see, hear, or touch. You can even be disgusted by ideas!

What color would you choose for disgust? Color in the circle with that color. Then, draw a picture about feeling disgusted using only that color.

What do you know about feeling disgusted? _____

_____

_____

_____

Name: _____　**Date:** _____

I feel disgusted! I also feel...

Here are some other words for feeling disgusted:

Sick　　　　　　Upset

When you feel disgusted, you might also feel:

Bored　　　　　Scared　　　　　Uneasy

You can be disgusted by a bad taste or a piece of trash. Disgust can be a small feeling or a big one!

Can you think of a time you felt disgusted? Draw a picture about it here.

Circle the face that is the closest to how you felt.

What do you usually do when you are disgusted? _____

_____

_____

Name: _____ **Date:** _____

What does disgust look like?

Some people show their disgust on their face. They might wrinkle their nose or close their eyes. Others may yell and scream about it.

How do you think a disgusted person looks and acts?

When someone is disgusted, what does their voice sound like? _____

_____

_____

_____

What does their face look like? Draw a picture of someone who is disgusted.

How do they act? What do they do with their body? _____

_____

_____

_____

Name: _____   Date: _____

Which is worse?

Does everyone find the same things disgusting? You are about to find out.

Find a partner. Ask each other which of the things below is worse. Circle the answer your partner chooses. Put an "X" next to the one you would choose.

Then switch and find a new partner. Ask the same questions. Use a different color to record their answers.

Which is worse?		
Smell something bad	OR	Taste something bad
Get your hands dirty	OR	Get your feet dirty
Hold a worm	OR	Hold a beetle
See someone pick their nose	OR	Hear someone blow their nose
Chewing on a pencil	OR	Chewing gum

Name: _____ **Date:** _____

How do you feel today? Circle each face that matches your feelings. Or draw your own.

Excited   Left Out   Sad   Calm   _____

What do you do when you feel disgusted?

You might scrunch up your nose like you smelled something bad. You might roll your eyes. You might take a step away from whatever is disgusting.

Think about the last time you felt disgusted. What happened? Draw a picture about it.

When I feel disgusted, my face looks like this:

When I feel disgusted, this is where I feel it in my body:

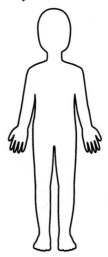

Name: _____ Date: _____

That's SO gross!

What makes you feel disgusted?

Write down something that you think is disgusting in each box. Then rate how disgusting each one is.

When you're done, find a partner and share your answers. Whose is the grossest?

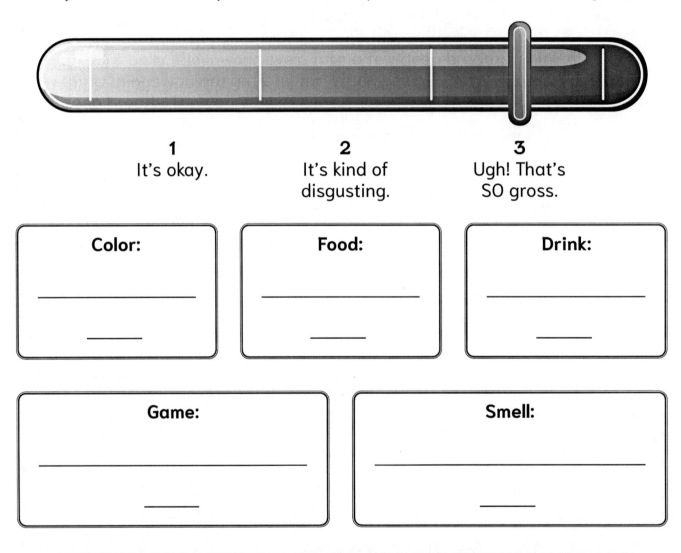

1
It's okay.

2
It's kind of
disgusting.

3
Ugh! That's
SO gross.

Color:
_____

___

Food:
_____

___

Drink:
_____

___

Game:
_____

___

Smell:
_____

___

Yoga Break

Does your belly hurt when you feel disgusted? Butterfly Pose is perfect for an upset belly. Sit down. Bend your knees. Bring the bottoms of your feet together. Sit up tall and place your hands on your ankles. Close your eyes if you like. Take at least three deep breaths.

Name: _____ **Date:** _____

Now and Then

Just like our other feelings, disgust has an important job to do. It's there to keep us safe.

Disgust reminds you not to eat rotten food. It can get you to back away from something that smells bad in case it might hurt you.

But not everything that disgusts you is dangerous. Disgust is a feeling that passes, just like any other. What used to disgust you may not anymore!

Draw a picture of something that used to disgust you.

Why do you now think it's not so bad? _____

_____

_____

Draw a picture of something that still disgusts you.

You don't have to avoid everything you think is gross. You might be disgusted by a vegetable, but it's still good for you!

Name: _____   **Date:** _____

How curious!

Sometimes we feel disgusted about something we have never even tried before.

Let's say broccoli disgusts you. Even though you only tried it once!

What if you were curious instead? You could taste one small bite. Maybe it will still be disgusting! But maybe it won't be so bad.

Draw a picture to answer each prompt. Write what it is underneath.

Something I think is disgusting but I've never tried:

_____

A food I think is gross but I've never tasted:

_____

A place that seems disgusting but I've never been to:

_____

Now choose one of your answers from above to answer these prompts.

I'm curious to learn more about: _____

This is who I will ask about it: _____

Name: _____   **Date:** _____

A Disgusting Story

What if you used your feeling of disgust as a clue?

Maybe it's a clue to be curious.

Maybe it's a warning to be safe.

Or maybe your disgust is a clue to take action.

For example, if you see someone getting bullied and it disgusts you, you can speak up. You can also ask an adult for help.

If someone says something disgusting, you can walk away. You can also laugh it off!

Make a short story about something that disgusts you. Draw or write what you could do about it. Use the prompts to inspire your story!

Ewww! This is disgusting.

Maybe there is something I could do to change it.

Aha! This will do the trick.

Next time, I'll do this instead.

Name: _____   **Date:** _____

How do you feel today? Circle each face that matches your feelings. Or draw your own.

Disgusted   Left Out   Upset   Loved   _____

Here's what I know now about disgust:

When I feel disgusted, I'm thinking… _____

_____

_____

_____

_____

When I am disgusted, I'm feeling… _____

_____

_____

_____

_____

Mindful Moment

If you're feeling really disgusted, some simple breathing can help you shift your mind. Take a deep breath in through your nose. Seal your lips together. As you breathe out make the sound of "Mmmmmmmm," like a buzzing bee. Repeat four times. Then go back to your regular breath.

Name: _____   Date: _____

What does it mean to feel embarrassed?

When you say, **"I feel embarrassed,"** you might be feeling a little shy. You might also feel a little ashamed, like you did something wrong.

What color would you choose for embarrassment? Color in the circle with that color. Then, draw a picture about feeling embarrassed using only that color.

What do you know about feeling embarrassed? _____

_____

_____

_____

Name: _____   **Date:** _____

I feel embarrassed! I also feel...

Here are some other words for feeling embarrassed:

Ashamed   Uneasy   Shy

When you feel embarrassed, you might also feel:

Hurt   Anxious   Frustrated

If you're feeling a little embarrassed, you could just laugh it off.

If you're feeling really embarrassed, that's okay too. You should ask for help if you're hurt.

Think of a time you felt embarrassed. What happened? _____

_____

_____

Circle the face that is the closest to how you felt.

How do you usually act when you are embarrassed? _____

_____

_____

Name: _____ **Date:** _____

How do people act when they are embarrassed?

Some people can just laugh about it. Others may be really upset. They might cry or get very quiet.

What does embarrassment look like to you?

When someone is embarrassed, what does their voice sound like? _____

_____

_____

_____

What does their face look like? Draw a picture of someone who is embarrassed.

How do they act? What do they do with their body? _____

_____

_____

_____

Name: _____　　Date: _____

Friendly Words

What do you say if a friend is feeling embarrassed?

Circle what you would say to a friend below. Remember that kindness is always the best choice!

A friend fell in front of the whole class.

Would you say:

Are you okay?　　　　　That was so funny!
Come sit by me.

A friend has something on their face.

Would you say:

Eww, that's so gross!　　　You have something on
　　　　　　　　　　　　　your face. Do you want
　　　　　　　　　　　　　some help?

A friend said a word wrong and someone laughed at them.

Would you say:

That's not how you say it!　　　That's okay, that
　　　　　　　　　　　　　　is a hard word.

Name: _____ **Date:** _____

How do you feel today? Circle each face that matches your feelings. Or draw your own.

Shy   Angry   Happy   Sad   _____

How do you know if you're embarrassed?

Your face might get red. You might feel very shy. Or you might cry or want to yell.

What happens when you feel embarrassed?

When I feel embarrassed, I... _____

_____

_____

When I am embarrassed, my face looks like this:

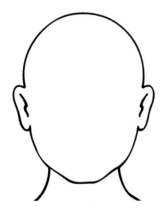

When I feel embarrassed, this is where I feel it in my body:

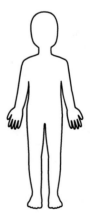

Mindful Moment

If you're embarrassed, take a deep breath! It helps you move on to the next feeling. Take a big breath in through your nose. Open your mouth and make a big *aaaahhhhh* sound as you breathe out. Do this a few times and you will feel better.

Name: _____   **Date:** _____

Does this embarrass you?

What makes you feel embarrassed? It's different for everyone.

Read each one of these. Would it embarrass you? Color in the face that matches how you would feel.

    You fall and rip your pants.

    You burp and it's loud.

    You forgot to tie your shoes.

    Everyone is staring at you.

Name: _____   **Date:** _____

Horn of the Unicorn

Do you ever feel embarrassed by yourself?

Maybe you have an extra-long pinky toe. Or a scratchy voice that you're shy about.

Those things are what make us each special. Like the horn of a unicorn! It's special.

Let's talk about what makes you special. Write your answer on each section of the unicorn's horn. Then color it in!

I'm _____ and this is what makes me special.

(your name)

I'm proud of _____

I'm good at _____

I can _____

Name: _____   **Date:** _____

When you are feeling embarrassed, you could just laugh it off.

At first, it may not seem funny at all. But maybe…it could be?

Of course, if you are hurt, it's not funny at all, you should ask for help.

Match up each embarrassing moment with a funny one.

You drop all of your   Take a bow.
stuff on the floor.

                              Laugh and say, "Oops!"

You call your teacher   Smile and wave.
the wrong name.

                              Tell a joke.

Someone catches
you staring at them.   Make a funny face.

                              Do a little dance.

You walk into the
wrong classroom.   Just smile.

Name: _____ **Date:** _____

How embarrassing!

Read this story and then answer the questions.

Ashley and Selena are getting a treat. Hooray for ice cream! But Ashley drops hers. It hits her shirt and leaves a big stain. And her ice cream is on the floor! Ashley starts to cry.

How do you think Ashley is feeling? _____

_____

_____

What should Selena say to Ashley? _____

_____

_____

What would you do if you were Ashley? _____

_____

_____

Draw a picture of how you think the story should end.

Name: _____　**Date:** _____

How do you feel today? Circle each face that matches your feelings. Or draw your own.

Anxious　　　Happy　　　Calm　　　Sad　　_____

Here's what I know now about embarrassment:

Next time I feel embarrassed, I will... _____

_____

_____

_____

_____

Here's what I would say to a friend when they are feeling embarrassed: _____

_____

_____

_____

_____

Yoga Break

Upward Facing Dog Pose is perfect for moving forward. Lie on your belly. Place your hands flat on the ground near your shoulders. Push your chest off the ground. Straighten your arms. Take three long, deep breaths.

Name: _____ Date: _____

What does it mean to feel excited?

When you say **"I feel excited,"** you are feeling happy. You can't wait for what is next!

What color would you choose for excitement? Color in the circle with that color. Then, draw a picture about feeling excited using only that color.

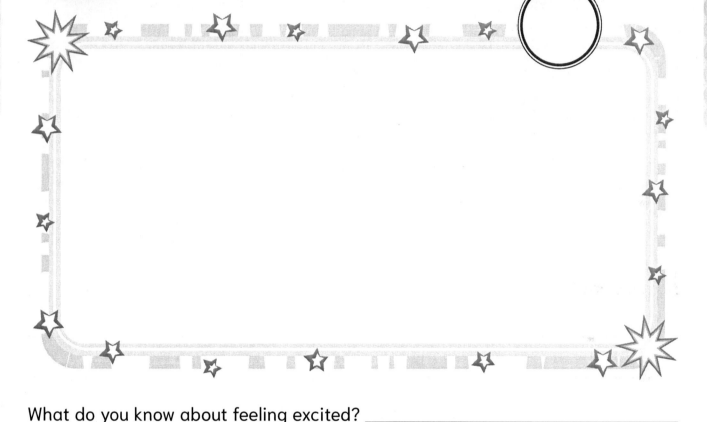

What do you know about feeling excited? _____

_____

_____

_____

Yoga Break

Try Horse Pose when you are feeling excited. Stand with your feet wide apart. Bend your knees. Turn your palms up. Take a long, deep breath.

Name: _____ Date: _____

I feel excited! I also feel...

Here are some other words for feeling excited:

Thrilled

Happy

Joyful

When you feel excited, you might also feel:

Nervous

Scared

Silly

Draw a picture about the last time you felt excited.

Circle the face that is the closest to how you felt.

What makes you feel excited? _____

_____

_____

Name: _____ **Date:** _____

How do you feel today? Circle each face that matches your feelings. Or draw your own.

Sad   Brave   Shy   Worried   _____

Excitement can be big and loud. It can be quiet too.

What do you think excitement looks like?

When someone is excited, what does their voice sound like? _____

_____

_____

_____

What does their face look like? Draw a picture of someone who is excited.

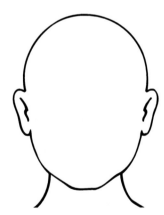

How do they act? What do they do with their body? _____

_____

_____

_____

Warm-Up 94   Unit 10: Excited

Name: _____   **Date:** _____

Party Time

This weekend is Olivia's birthday party. She can't wait to see all of her friends.

Olivia daydreams all day about her party. She thinks about how her cake will taste. What games will they play? She even wonders about the gifts she might get.

You sit next to Olivia in class. You can see she is not listening. She won't stop talking about her party. And she is staring off into space!

How do you think Olivia is feeling? _____

_____

_____

_____

What would you say to Olivia to help her stay focused until the party?

_____

_____

_____

Draw a picture of how you think the story ends.

#9096 Daily Warm-Ups: Social-Emotional Reflections   ©*Teacher Created Resources*

Name: _____ **Date:** _____

Excitement is great, isn't it?

Does your heart beat a bit faster when you are excited? Does your belly rumble?

What does excitement feel like for you?

What gets you excited? _____

_____

_____

_____

When I am excited, my face looks like this:

When I feel excited, this is where I feel it in my body:

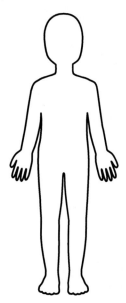

When I am excited, I also feel... _____

_____

_____

_____

Name: _____   **Date:** _____

What to Do

What makes you feel excited? What calms you down?

Color in the items below. Then cut them out and paste them where they fit for you.

This makes me feel excited	This makes me feel calm

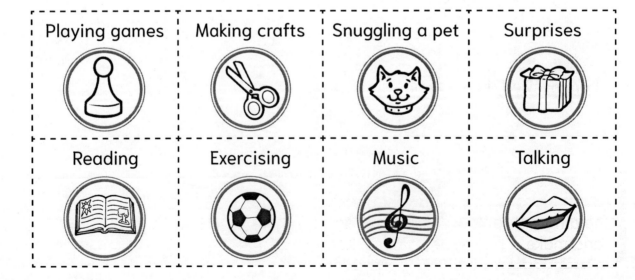

Name: _____   **Date:** _____

Be Cool

It can be hard to focus when you are excited.

That's when it's time to be cool! Take a deep breath. Then you can focus again.

Name one thing you are excited about. _____

Why are you excited? _____

_____

_____

_____

What is one thing you can do to calm down if you get too excited?

_____

_____

_____

Mindful Moment

Bubble Breath can help when you are too excited. Pretend you are holding a bubble wand in your hand. Take a deep breath. Blow out and make a bunch of bubbles. Keep going!

Name: _____   Date: _____

Get Excited

Have you ever had to do something you didn't want to? We all have. It can make us grumpy!

That's when feeling excited can help. A little bit of excitement can make the grumpiness go away.

Draw a picture of something you didn't want to do.

How did you feel? _____

_____

_____

Pretend you can go back in time. This time you can add a little excitement.

Draw a picture of what would happen!

Name: _____   **Date:** _____

Wishes and Dreams

Let's get excited about the future!

Draw your answers to these questions.

Where will you live?

Where do you want to visit someday?

What will you invent?

Who will be your best friend?

Name: _____ **Date:** _____

How do you feel today? Circle each face that matches your feelings. Or draw your own.

Left Out   Shy   Happy   Silly   _____

What do you know now about feeling excited? _____

_____

_____

_____

Next time I'm feeling excited, I am going to remember… _____

_____

_____

_____

Draw a picture of the most exciting thing you can imagine.

Name: _____ **Date:** _____

What is frustration?

Frustration happens when we try really hard but we can't do it.

It's when we wish we could change it, but we can't.

When things aren't going our way, we may feel frustrated. We say, **"I feel frustrated."**

What color would you choose for frustration? Color in the circle with that color. Then, draw a picture about feeling frustrated using only that color.

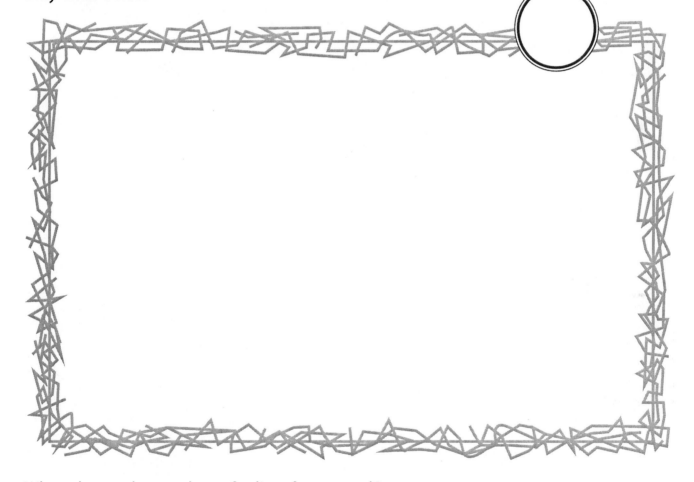

What do you know about feeling frustrated? _____

_____

_____

_____

Name: _____   Date: _____

I feel frustrated! I also feel...

Here are some other words for feeling frustrated:

Mad

Irritated

Hurt

When you feel frustrated, you might also feel:

Down

Sad

Upset

We all get frustrated from time to time. It's okay! Things don't always go the way we want.

Can you think of a time you felt frustrated? Draw a picture about it here.

Circle the face that is the closest to how you felt.

What do you usually do when you are frustrated? _____

_____

_____

Name: _____   **Date:** _____

What does frustration look like?

Some people keep it all inside. You might never even know they are frustrated. Other people express it loudly. They might yell or be mad.

When someone is frustrated, what does their voice sound like? _____

_____

_____

_____

What does their face look like? Draw a picture of someone who is frustrated.

How do they act? What do they do with their body? _____

_____

_____

_____

Mindful Moment

Feeling frustrated? Take a breath! Press your thumb and index finger together. Take a deep breath in and out. Keep going, as long as you want.

Name: _____   Date: _____

A Fox with No Socks

There is a fox who has lost his socks. He looks everywhere. But he can't find his socks!

Now his den is a mess. And his socks are nowhere to be found.

How do you think the fox feels? _____

_____

_____

What would you tell him? _____

_____

_____

Draw a picture
of what the fox
could do next.

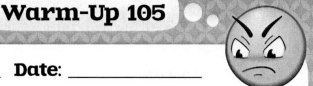

Name: _____ **Date:** _____

How do you feel today? Circle each face that matches your feelings. Or draw your own.

Brave   Sad   Stressed   Loved   _____

What happens when you are feeling frustrated?

You might feel mad or sad. Or maybe you get very quiet.

When is the last time you felt frustrated? Draw a picture about what happened.

When I feel frustrated, my face looks like this:

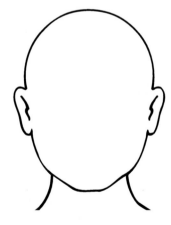

When I feel frustrated, this is where I feel it in my body:

When I feel frustrated, I also feel... _____

_____

_____

Name: _____   Date: _____

This is hard.

Do you ever feel frustrated when things get hard? It's okay if you do.

Rate what frustrates you. Make an *X* in the column that matches your answer.

	Very Frustrating	A Little Frustrating	Not Frustrating
1. Listening			
2. Art			
3. Exercise			
4. Math			
5. Music			
6. Reading			
7. Science			
8. Sharing			

Name: _____ **Date:** _____

Find a Way

Frustrating stuff happens. It's just a part of life! What matters is how you deal with it.

Imagine you are walking along and you discover a huge rock in your path. It's so big! You can't see around it.

What will you do? How will you keep going on your path?

Draw a picture of yourself and the rock and what you would do. Then explain your picture below.

Here's how I found a way to keep going on my path: _____

_____

_____

_____

Name: _____   Date: _____

Three Stars and Three Wishes

Sometimes it feels like you can't do anything right. That can be frustrating!

Everyone has things they are good at. We also have things we would like to do better.

Write or draw your answers to the questions below.

What are three things you are good at?

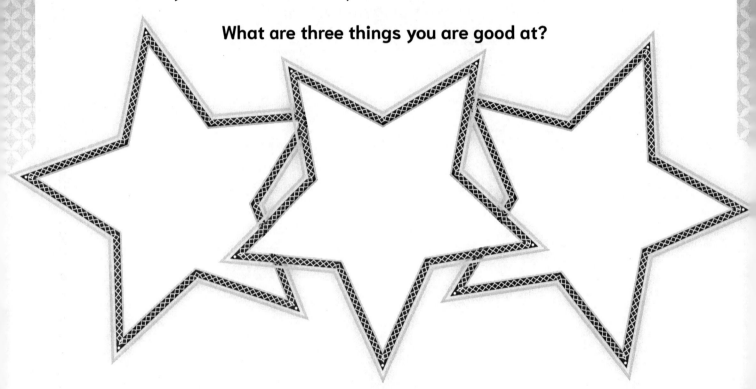

What are three things you would like to do better?

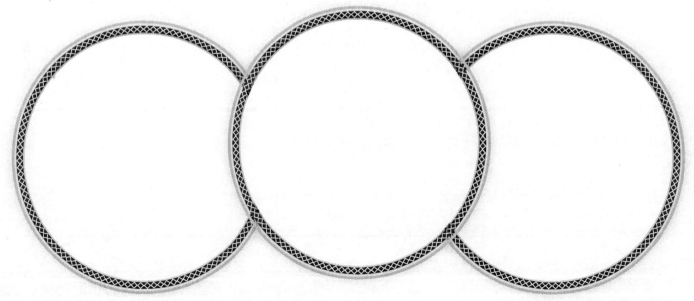

Name: _____ **Date:** _____

Get Gritty

When you get frustrated, don't give up! Keep trying, and find your *GRIT*.

GRIT stands for:	• **G** • Give it your all.
	• **R** • Redo if necessary.
	• **I** • Ignore giving up.
	• **T** • Take time to do it right.

Think about a time when you wanted to give up. Draw a picture about it here.

Instead of giving up, what is one thing you could do? _____

_____

_____

_____

Name: _____   **Date:** _____

How do you feel today? Circle each face that matches your feeling. Or draw your own.

Goofy   Proud   Tired   Shy   _____

Here's what I know now about frustration:

Next time I feel frustrated, I will try… _____

_____

_____

_____

_____

_____

Here's what I will say to myself: _____

_____

_____

_____

_____

Yoga Break

Try Cat Pose the next time you feel like giving up. Start on your hands and knees. Press your hands into the ground. Round your back like a scared cat. Take three deep breaths.

Name: _____   **Date:** _____

What does it mean to feel happy?

When you say, **"I feel happy,"** you're feeling good. You smile a lot. You are in a good mood!

What color would you choose for happiness? Color in the circle with that color. Then, draw a picture about feeling happy using only that color.

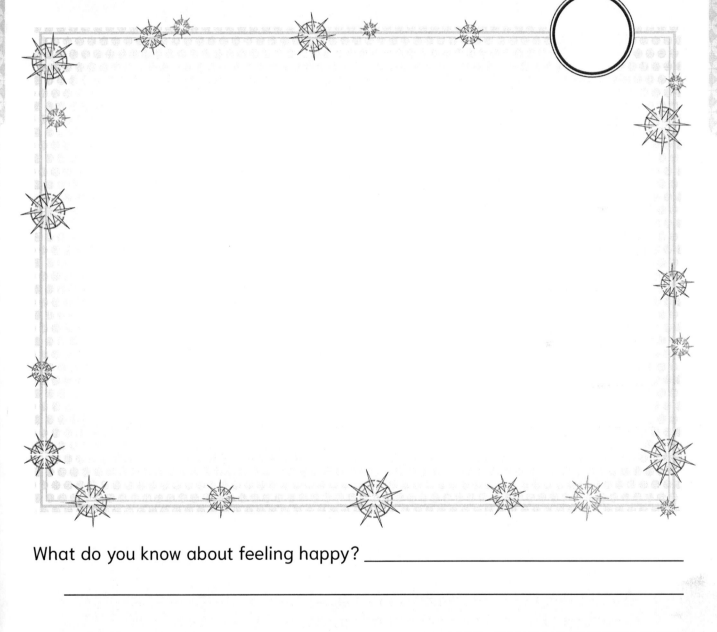

What do you know about feeling happy? _____

_____

_____

Name: _____　**Date:** _____

I feel happy! I also feel...

Here are some other words for feeling happy:

Joyful　　　　　　Smiling　　　　　　Cheery

When you feel happy, you might also feel:

Loved　　　　　　Confident　　　　　　Excited

Draw a picture of the last time you felt happy.

Circle the face that is the closest to how you felt.

Why do you think you felt happy? _____

_____

_____

Name: _____   **Date:** _____

How can you tell when someone is happy?

A happy person might have a big smile. They may laugh a lot. They are fun to be around!

When someone is happy, what does their voice sound like? _____

_____

_____

_____

What does their face look like? Draw a picture of someone who is happy.

How do they act? What do they do with their body? _____

_____

_____

_____

Yoga Break

Try Happy Baby Pose to feel happy right away! Lie on your back. Pull your knees in. Grab your feet. Then gently rock back and forth.

Name: _____   **Date:** _____

Make Someone Happy

What if you had the power to make people happy?

Imagine you have a magic wand. Wave it and you can make a person happy.

Who would you use your power on?

_____

Draw a picture of what you would do to make them happy.

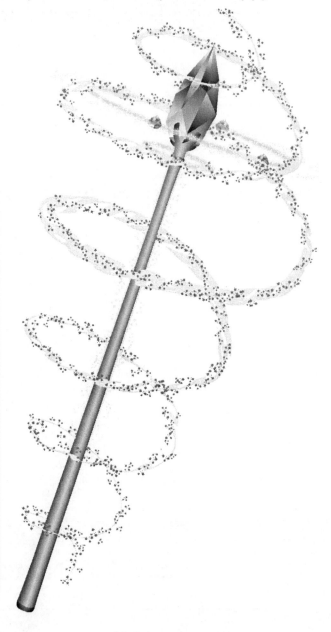

How would they act? What would they do? _____

_____

_____

Name: _____ **Date:** _____

How do you feel today? Circle each face that matches your feelings. Or draw your own.

Shy   Tired   Happy   Sad   _____

How does it look and feel when you are happy?

Do you smile? Do you giggle? Do you do a happy dance?

When I feel happy, my face looks like this:

When I'm happy, this is where I feel it in my body:

When I feel happy, I might also be feeling... _____

_____

_____

Name: _____   Date: _____

What makes you happy?

What makes you happier? Color in your answer.

Rainy Days   OR   Sunny Days

Pancakes   OR   Ice Cream

Dogs   OR   Cats

Playing Outside   OR   Playing Inside

Dancing   OR   Singing

What makes you the happiest of all? _____

_____

Name: _____ Date: _____

My Happy Place

Imagine a place that is just yours. Every single thing there makes you feel happy. This is your happy place!

What would your happy place look like? What colors are there? Who else is there?

Draw your happy place below.

My Happy Place

What do you do in your happy place? _____

_____

_____

Name: _____   Date: _____

Spread Happiness

Happiness is everywhere! Can you find it?

Once you start looking around, you can see happiness all around you.

The more happiness you find, the happier you'll feel!

Draw a happy animal.

Draw a happy bug.

Draw a happy flower.

Draw a happy vegetable.

So Thankful

Name: _____   **Date:** _____

If you are ever feeling down, try this.

Remember what you are thankful for. Even when you are sad, feeling thankful can make you smile.

I am thankful for

because...

Mindful Moment

When you feel thankful, it can help you feel happy! Close your eyes. Take a deep breath. Think about one thing you are thankful for. Take at least three more deep breaths. Then open your eyes.

Name: _____ **Date:** _____

How do you feel today? Circle each face that matches your feelings. Or draw your own.

  Brave   Calm   Proud   Scared   _____

Here's what I know now about feeling happy:

When I'm happy, I'm thinking… _____

_____

_____

_____

When I'm happy, I'm feeling… _____

_____

_____

Draw a picture of yourself doing something that makes you happy.

Name: _____ Date: _____

What is jealousy?

We say, **"I feel jealous"** when we wish we had what someone else has.

What color would you choose for jealousy? Color in the circle with that color. Then, draw a picture about feeling jealous using only that color.

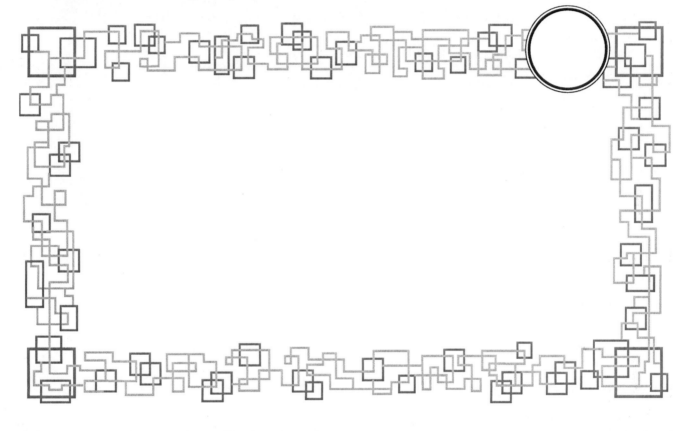

What do you know about feeling jealous? _____

_____

_____

Mindful Moment

If you feel jealous, try Box Breath. Take a deep breath in and count 1–2–3–4. Hold it and count 1–2–3–4. Slowly breathe out and count 1–2–3–4. Hold again and count 1–2–3–4. Keep going!

Name: _____   Date: _____

I feel jealous! I also feel...

Here are some other words for feeling jealous:

Envious   Greedy   Bitter

When you feel jealous, you might also feel:

Sad   Upset   Worried

It's okay to feel jealous sometimes. Everyone does! But it's not okay to act out.

Draw a picture about the last time you felt jealous.

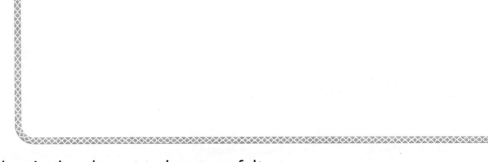

Circle the face that is the closest to how you felt.

How do you usually act when you're feeling jealous? _____

_____

_____

Name: _____ **Date:** _____

How can you tell when someone is jealous?

Can you see it in their face? Or hear it in what they say?

When someone is jealous, what does their voice sound like? _____

_____

_____

_____

What does their face look like? Draw a picture of someone who is jealous.

How do they act? What do they do with their body? _____

_____

_____

_____

Name: _____   **Date:** _____

How do you feel today? Circle each face that matches your feelings. Or draw your own.

Bored   Excited   Shy   Nervous   _____

How you act when you are jealous might be different from how a friend acts.

Find a partner and help each other answer these questions. Draw your partner's answers.

> ### What makes you feel jealous?

> ### How do you act when you are jealous?

Warm-Up 125

Name: _____   **Date:** _____

What does it look and feel like when you are jealous?

What makes you feel jealous? _____

_____

_____

_____

When I feel jealous, my face looks like this:

When I'm jealous, this is where I feel it in my body:

When I feel jealous, I might also be feeling... _____

_____

_____

_____

Yoga Break

When you are feeling jealous, try this Frog Pose. Stand with your feet wide apart. Bend your knees and squat. Bring your hands together in front of your chest. Take at least three deep breaths.

Name: _____ Date: _____

Jelly Beans

What makes you "jelly"? Color the jelly beans next to what would make you jealous.

 A friend has a new toy you want.

 Your friend has a new friend.

 Someone gets to cut in line.

 No one is listening to you.

 Someone else gets picked.

Name: _____   **Date:** _____

The Jealous Monster

Jealousy can make us say and do things we feel bad about later.

Think of jealousy as a big, hairy monster that takes over your brain for a few minutes.

Color your own Jealous Monster. Then write your answers to the prompts below.

My name is _____

_____

I like to eat... _____

_____

_____

_____

I show up when... _____

_____

_____

_____

Name: _____   Date: _____

How Do They Feel?

Jealousy comes with other feelings too. Feeling sad or mad is okay!

Read each situation. Color in the faces that match what you think each person might be feeling.

Sophia's friends had a party without her. Sophia is feeling...

   and

Jealous   Sad   Hurt   Mad

Elijah's friend always scores more than Elijah does in soccer. Elijah is feeling...

   and

Jealous   Happy   Upset   Sad

Mason's family is welcoming a new baby. Mason is feeling...

   and

Jealous   Excited   Hurt   Afraid

Jacob's best friend just got a puppy. Jacob is feeling...

   and

Jealous   Sad   Mad   Excited

You're Number One!

Name: _____ **Date:** _____

When you're feeling jealous, remember to be proud of yourself. You are already amazing!

What are some of the things you are proud of?

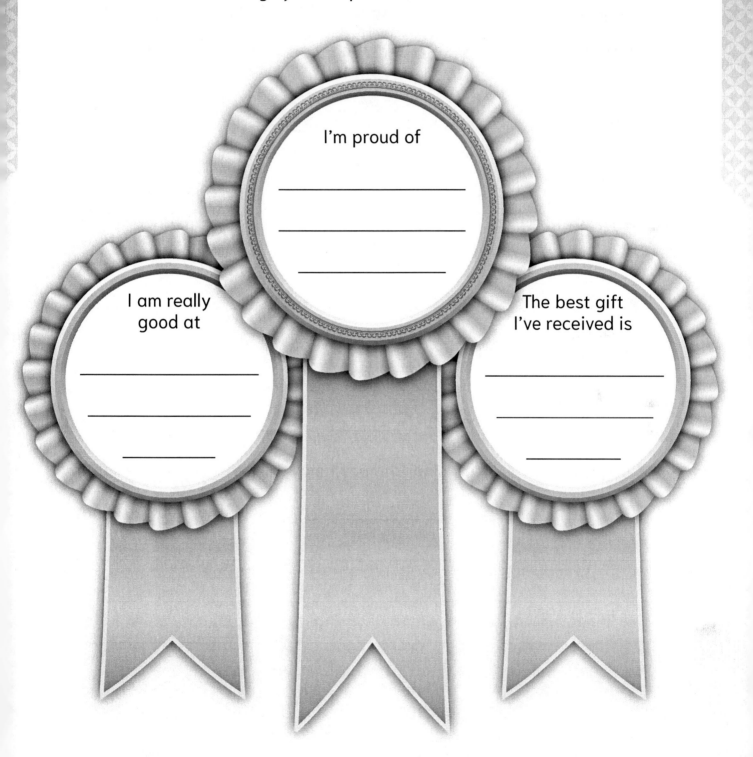

I'm proud of

_____

_____

_____

I am really good at

_____

_____

_____

The best gift I've received is

_____

_____

_____

Name: _____   **Date:** _____

How do you feel today? Circle each face that matches your feelings. Or draw your own.

Silly   Angry   Happy   Bored   _____

Here's what I know now about feeling jealous:

When I'm jealous, my brain is saying… _____

_____

_____

_____

When I'm jealous, I feel… _____

_____

_____

_____

Draw a picture of what you will do the next time you feel jealous.

Name: _____ **Date:** _____

What does it mean to feel left out?

We feel left out when it feels like the good stuff is happening without us.

It can be a sad feeling.

You might say, **"I feel left out."**

What color would you choose for feeling left out? Color in the circle with that color. Then, draw a picture about feeling left out using only that color.

What do you know about feeling left out? _____

_____

_____

_____

Name: _____ Date: _____

I feel left out! I also feel...

Here are some other words for feeling left out:

Lonely   Sad   Down

When you feel left out, you might also feel:

Upset   Hurt   Angry

Everyone feels left out sometimes!

Think about a
time you felt
left out. Draw
a picture
about it.

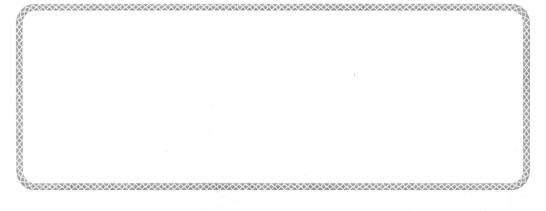

Circle the face that is the closest to how you felt.

Why do you think you felt left out? _____

_____

_____

Name: _____ **Date:** _____

How do you know if someone is feeling left out?

Someone who is feeling left out may look sad. They may want to be alone.

When someone is feeling left out, what does their voice sound like?

_____

_____

_____

What does their face look like? Draw a picture of someone who is feeling left out.

How do they act? What do they do with their body? _____

_____

_____

_____

Yoga Break

Next time you are feeling a little sad, try Bridge Pose. Lie on your back. Bend your knees and place your feet flat on the floor. Take a deep breath in. Lift your hips up. Stay for three breaths. Slowly come back down. Repeat a few times!

Name: _____　Date: _____

What's next?

Have you ever noticed someone else feeling left out? Did you try to help them?

When someone is feeling left out, it's nice to try to help.

In this exercise, you get to choose what will happen next. Draw or write your answers.

Bella's friends are playing a game she doesn't know.

How do you think Bella feels?

_____

_____

_____

_____

Draw a picture of what happens next.

Lucas tells Tyler a secret in front of Evan.

How do you think Evan feels?

_____

_____

_____

_____

Draw a picture of what happens next.

Name: _____ **Date:** _____

How do you feel today? Circle each face that matches your feelings. Or draw your own.

Worried   Afraid   Calm   Happy   _____

How does it feel when you are left out?

It might make you feel down or tired. It can make you mad too.

Think about the last time you were feeling left out. Draw a picture of what was happening.

When I feel left out, my face looks like this:

When I'm feeling left out, this is where I feel it in my body:

When I'm feeling left out, I might also be feeling... _____

_____

_____

Name: _____　**Date:** _____

Feeling Left Out

Let's talk more about feeling left out. Write your answers below.

Then find a partner and share your answers.

I feel left out when… _____

_____

_____

_____

When I feel left out, I… _____

_____

_____

_____

One thing I wish would happen when I feel left out: _____

_____

_____

_____

Mindful Moment

Try Buddy Breath with your partner. Sit on the floor back–to–back. Close your eyes and breathe. Take five slow, long breaths. Then open your eyes and turn back around. How did that feel?

Name: _____ Date: _____

Happy Thoughts

When you're feeling left out, you might be thinking sad thoughts.

But what if you changed your mind? You could think happy thoughts instead.

Let's practice. Choose a favorite word from under each box. Write it in the box.

Repeat these happy thoughts any time you need to!

I am

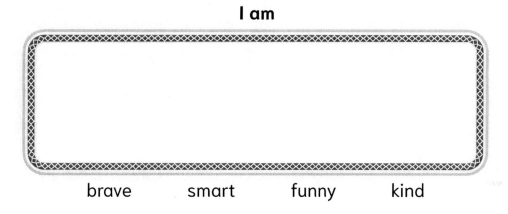

brave   smart   funny   kind

I

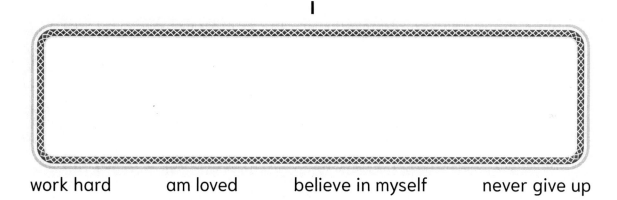

work hard   am loved   believe in myself   never give up

Today I will

have a great day   try my best   make good choices   be kind

Name: _____ **Date:** _____

Lonely Planet

Feeling left out is lonely. It can feel like you are on a planet all by yourself!

Next time you feel left out, what will you do?

Who can you talk to?

_____

_____

_____

What is one thing you can do to feel better?

_____

_____

_____

What is one happy thought you could have?

_____

_____

_____

Name: _____ **Date:** _____

We are kind.

When someone feels left out, it's the perfect time to be kind!

If you notice someone feeling left out, be kind.

And if you are feeling left out, be kind to someone else. It will help you feel better!

Let's practice some kindness.

A kind thing I
could say to a friend:

_____

_____

A kind thing I
could say to anyone:

_____

_____

A kind thing I
could do for someone:

_____

_____

A kind thing
someone has done for me:

_____

_____

Name: _____ **Date:** _____

How do you feel today? Circle each face that matches your feelings. Or draw your own.

Down   Nervous   Joyful   Calm   _____

Here's what I know now about feeling left out:

When I'm feeling left out, I'm thinking… _____

_____

_____

When I'm feeling left out, it feels like… _____

_____

_____

Next time I'm feeling left out, I'm going to remember… _____

_____

_____

Draw a picture of what you will do the next time you are feeling left out.

Name: _____ Date: _____

What does it mean to feel sad?

Sadness is the feeling we get when we have lost something.

When we say, **"I'm feeling sad,"** we might be feeling hurt or lonely too.

What color would you choose for sadness? Color in the circle with that color. Then, draw a picture about feeling sad using only that color.

What do you know about feeling sad? _____

_____

_____

Mindful Moment

When you're feeling sad, try Bunny Breath. Sit up tall. Breathe in with three short sniffs through your nose. Scrunch your nose up like a bunny! Then open your mouth and let the breath out slowly. Repeat at least five times.

Name: _____   Date: _____

I feel sad! I also feel...

Here are some other words for feeling sad:

Lonely   Down   Upset

When you feel sad, you might also feel:

Worried   Scared   Hurt

Draw a picture about the last time you felt sad.

Circle the face that is the closest to how you felt.

What was happening? _____

_____

_____

Sadness is something we all feel sometimes. If you're ever feeling sad for a long time, you should talk to a parent or a friend about it. Talking about it helps!

Name: _____ **Date:** _____

When we are sad, we sometimes cry. But we can be sad without crying too.

When someone is sad, their shoulders may slump. Or the corners of their mouth may turn down.

What do you think feeling sad looks like?

When someone is sad, what does their voice sound like? _____

_____

_____

What does their face look like? Draw a picture of someone who is sad.

How do they act? What do they do with their body? _____

_____

_____

How else do you know someone is sad? _____

_____

_____

Name: _____   **Date:** _____

How do you feel today? Circle each face that matches your feelings. Or draw your own.

    Left Out   Proud   Shy   Tired   _____

When you're feeling sad, it can feel like no one else understands.

Have you ever been a friend to someone who was feeling sad?

What would you say to a friend who is sad? _____

_____

_____

What is one thing you could do to cheer up a sad friend? _____

_____

_____

Draw a picture of yourself helping a sad friend.

When you're talking to a sad friend, listen carefully. If you have felt like they have before, say so! It can mean a lot to hear a friend say, "I know how that feels. I'm sorry."

Name: _____   **Date:** _____

How do you feel today? Circle each face that matches your feelings. Or draw your own.

Brave   Worried   Sad   Excited   _____

Did you know sadness has a job to do?

Sadness is like a signal that points to what we're feeling.

How do you act and feel when you are feeling sad?

When I feel sad, my face looks like this:

When I'm sad, this is where I feel it in my body:

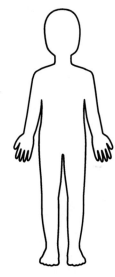

When I feel sad, I might also be feeling... _____

_____

_____

_____

Name: _____   **Date:** _____

That's so sad.

All kinds of things can make you sad. Big things and little things!

Have you ever felt sad about any of these things? Check the box if you have.

☐ You lost something.   ☐ You heard a sad song.

☐ You miss someone.   ☐ Your feelings got hurt.

☐ Someone was mean to you.   ☐ You felt left out.

Choose one of the answers you checked above and write about it here. What happened? Why were you sad?

_____

_____

_____

_____

_____

_____

_____

_____

_____

_____

_____

Upside-down Frown

When you're feeling sad, what would make you feel better?

Read these sad sentences. Then cut out and paste a bright idea that would help in each lightbulb.

You feel lonely.

You lost your favorite toy.

You are having a bad day.

You're missing someone.

You woke up grumpy.

Talk to a friend.

Write them a note.

Find something else to play with.

Think of something you're thankful for.

Take a few deep breaths.

Name: _____ **Date:** _____

Cheer Up

It's okay to feel sad. You don't have to rush to be happy again!

But when you are ready, you can choose one of these to cheer you up.

For each idea, draw a picture or symbol that will help you remember it.

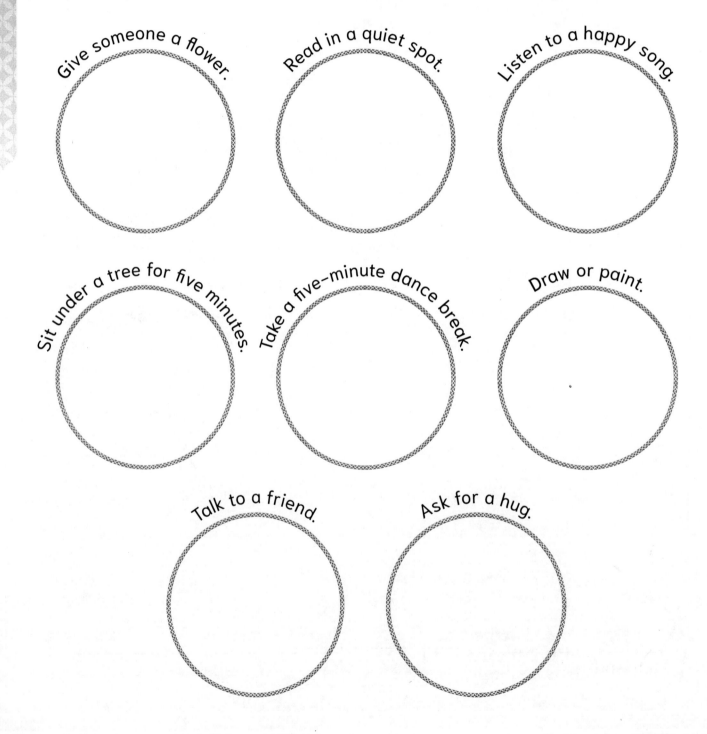

Give someone a flower.

Read in a quiet spot.

Listen to a happy song.

Sit under a tree for five minutes.

Take a five-minute dance break.

Draw or paint.

Talk to a friend.

Ask for a hug.

Name: _____ Date: _____

Sad to Happy

How do you go from feeling sad to feeling happy again?

Take the path to happy, and fill in what you will do next time you are sad.

1. Be Sad

Look for the signs that you are feeling sad. How will you know if you're sad?

_____

_____

2. Let It Be

Give yourself some time to feel sad. What are some other emotions you might feel too?

_____

_____

3. Buddy Up

Talk to a friend about how you feel, or ask for a hug. Who can help when you feel sad?

_____

_____

4. Help Yourself

You can move your body, get quiet, or rest. How will you help yourself feel better?

_____

_____

Name: _____ **Date:** _____

Here's what I know now about feeling sad:

When I'm sad, my brain is saying… _____

_____

_____

When I'm sad, I'm feeling… _____

_____

_____

Here's what I will do the next time I feel sad: _____

_____

_____

_____

Draw a picture of yourself helping a friend deal with sadness.

Yoga Break

Low Lunge Pose can help when you are sad. Start on your knees. Step your right foot forward. Lean your body forward. Lift your arms straight up. Take three deep breaths. Do the same on the other side.

Name: _____ **Date:** _____

What is shyness?

We say **"I feel shy"** when we're feeling unsure.

You might feel shy in a new place or meeting a new person.

What color would you choose for shyness? Color in the circle with that color. Then, draw a picture about feeling shy using only that color.

What do you know about feeling shy? _____

_____

_____

_____

Yoga Break

When you're feeling shy, Triangle Pose can help you feel brave. Stand with your feet wide apart. Stretch your arms straight out to the sides. Tilt over until your right fingers touch your right shin or ankle. Take three deep breaths, then switch to the other side.

Name: _____ **Date:** _____

I feel shy! I also feel...

Here are some other words for feeling shy:

Uncomfortable   Bashful   Nervous

When you feel shy, you might also feel:

Scared   Stressed   Worried

Think of the last time you felt shy. What happened? _____

_____

_____

_____

Circle the face that is the closest to how you felt.

How do you usually act when you are shy? _____

_____

_____

_____

Name: _____   **Date:** _____

Some people are very quiet when they feel shy. Others may tell you they are feeling shy.

What do you notice when someone is acting shy?

When someone is shy, what does their voice sound like? _____

_____

_____

What does their face look like? Draw a picture of someone who is shy.

How do they act? What do they do with their body? _____

_____

_____

_____

How else do you know someone is shy? _____

_____

_____

_____

Name: _____   **Date:** _____

Feeling Shy

Ellie starts a new school today. She doesn't know anyone there. Her new teacher asks her to stand up and tell the class about herself. Ellie stands, but she can't find her words. It feels like everyone is staring at her!

Color in the emotions Ellie might be feeling right now.

Shy   Embarrassed   Nervous   Uncomfortable

Circle some other feelings she might be having too.

Excited   Confident   Brave   Worried

Why do you think Ellie might be feeling that way? _____

_____

_____

_____

_____

If you were Ellie's friend, what would you say to her? _____

_____

_____

_____

_____

Name: _____ **Date:** _____

How do you feel today? Circle each face that matches your feelings. Or draw your own.

Disgusted   Calm   Hurt   Silly   _____

How do you know if you're feeling shy?

You might feel butterflies in your stomach. Or you might feel like you can't speak.

How does shyness feel for you?

When I feel shy, my face looks like this:

When I feel shy, this is where I feel it in my body:

 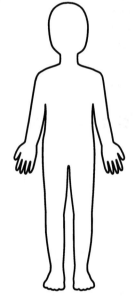

When I feel shy, I also feel... _____

_____

_____

_____

Name: _____   **Date:** _____

Shy or not?

What makes you feel shy?

For each of these, color in the face that matches how you would feel.

Your teacher asks you to read.

You meet someone new.

Someone asks you a question.

You have to ask an adult a question.

Mindful Moment

When you're feeling shy, try Flower Breath. Close your eyes and imagine you are smelling a sweet flower. Hold your breath and count to three. Then let the breath out through your mouth, like you're blowing the fuzz off a dandelion. Repeat three times. Then open your eyes.

Name: _____   **Date:** _____

Hold On Please

It's always okay to feel shy.

And it's also okay to take a moment before you decide how you feel. If you take a few deep breaths, you might feel less shy.

Here are a few things you could say when you are feeling shy. Draw a picture to go with each one.

"I'm not sure."

"Just a moment, please."

"I'm feeling a little shy."

Name: _____   Date: _____

Imagine This

When you are feeling shy, it can seem hard to be brave. But what if you closed your eyes and pretended you were brave?

The more you see yourself as a brave person, the braver you can be!

Pretend you are asked to talk to a room full of people. You don't know anyone in the room.

But you are very brave!

Draw a picture
about what
would happen.

What would you say to yourself to feel braver? _____

_____

_____

_____

Name: _____ **Date:** _____

Hi, I'm Shy.

Do you know what makes you feel shy?

Shyness can be sneaky. Sometimes we feel it all of a sudden! Other times, we can feel it coming.

What brings out your shyness?

What is one thing that makes you feel shy? _____

_____

_____

Why do you think it makes you feel shy? _____

_____

_____

Draw a picture of something that makes you feel brave.

What would you say to a friend who is feeling shy? _____

_____

_____

Warm-Up 160   Unit 16: Shy

Name: _____   **Date:** _____

How do you feel today? Circle each face that matches your feelings. Or draw your own.

Sad   Calm   Goofy   Left Out   _____

Here's what I know now about feeling shy:

When I'm feeling shy, I'm thinking…. _____

_____

_____

_____

When I'm feeling shy, I'm feeling… _____

_____

_____

_____

Draw a picture of something you used to feel shy about.

Name: _____   **Date:** _____

How are you feeling?

Now that you know a bit more about your feelings, can you picture them?

Fill in the blanks on these funny faces. Draw the missing faces. Name the faces that are already here with feelings. Color each one to match the feeling.

Disgusted   _____   Angry

_____   _____   Shy

Bored   Excited   _____

Name: _____   Date: _____

In the Zones

Some feelings are like each other. Feeling very excited is kind of like feeling very worried. Feeling sad is like feeling bored.

Here, we will put feelings into zones. Read the zones below, and color them in. Then draw a face to match each one.

Blue

Draw a face to match these feelings.

Green

Draw a face to match these feelings.

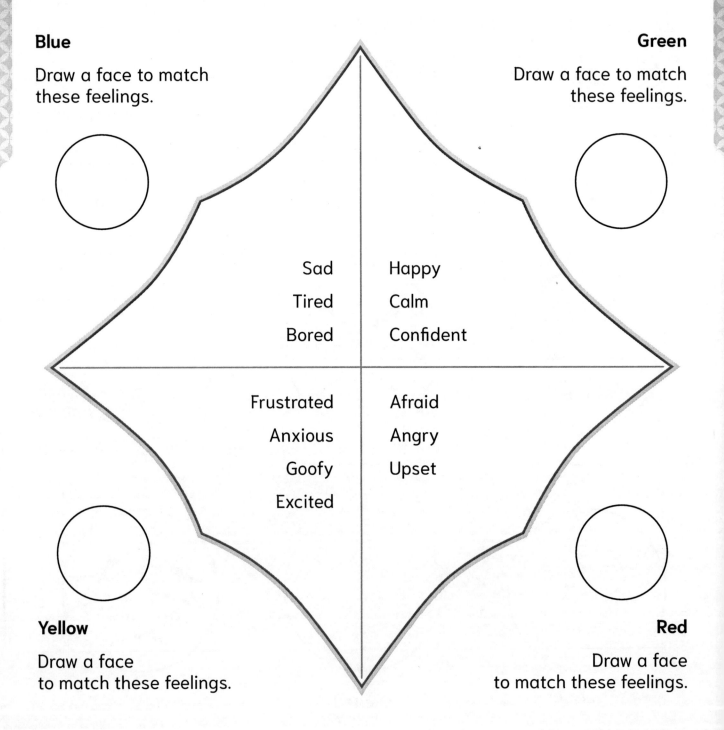

Sad   Happy

Tired   Calm

Bored   Confident

Frustrated   Afraid

Anxious   Angry

Goofy   Upset

Excited

Yellow

Draw a face to match these feelings.

Red

Draw a face to match these feelings.

Name: _____ **Date:** _____

Clued-in to Feelings

Something good or bad just happened to you. You notice a feeling. What is it?

Just like a detective, you can look for clues. You may find clues in your body or your face. You may find clues in the way others react to you.

Read each clue. Name the feeling you think it might be and why you think that.

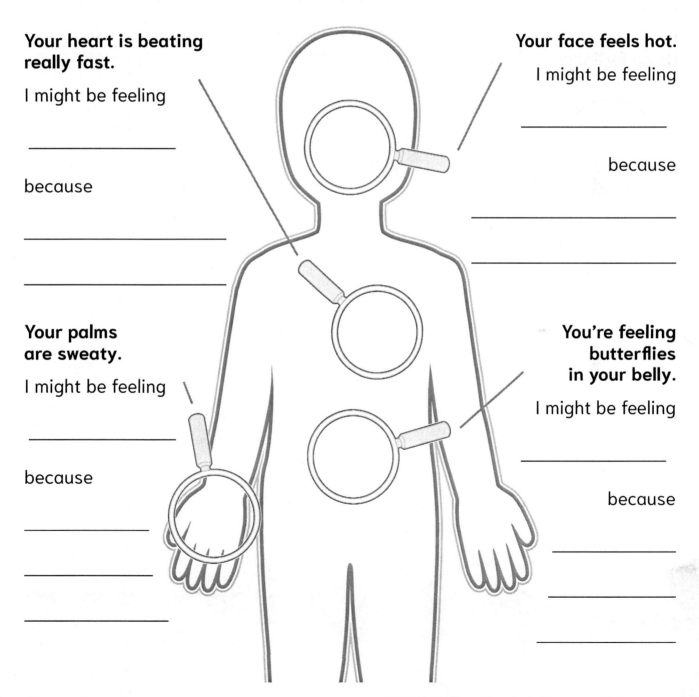

Your heart is beating really fast.

I might be feeling

_____

because

_____

_____

Your face feels hot.

I might be feeling

_____

because

_____

_____

Your palms are sweaty.

I might be feeling

_____

because

_____

_____

You're feeling butterflies in your belly.

I might be feeling

_____

because

_____

_____

_____

Name: _____   Date: _____

A Rainbow of Feelings

Did you know you can feel a bunch of different feelings at the same time?

Think of your feelings like a rainbow. There is more than just one color! Just like you can have more than one feeling at the same time.

Read the sentence for each rainbow. Then color in the feelings.

Red = Angry	Orange = Afraid	Yellow = Worried	Green = Happy	Blue = Sad	Purple = Calm

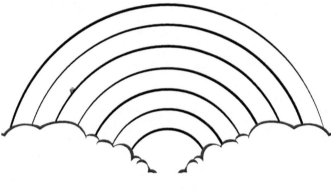

Hannah waves "hi" to her friend Lucy. But Lucy doesn't wave back. How does Hannah feel?

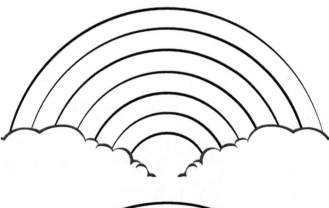

Your lucky socks are missing! You think you will never see them again. But then you find them at the back of your sock drawer. How are you feeling?

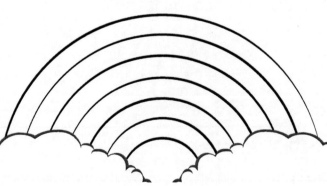

Today is Landon's birthday. But his belly hurts and he wants to take a nap. How does he feel?

Name: _____ **Date:** _____

Feelings Big and Small

How do you feel today? Fill in the faces with how you are feeling and name the feelings.

_____   _____   _____

Have you ever heard someone say, "I'm feeling a little sad today." Or maybe, "I'm really angry right now!"

Sometimes our feelings are BIG. Then the big feeling is all we can think about.

Sometimes our feelings are small. You might not even know you are having a small feeling.

What are some of your big and small feelings?

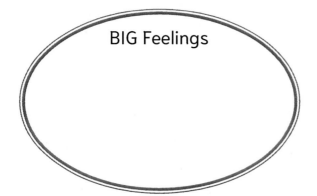
BIG Feelings

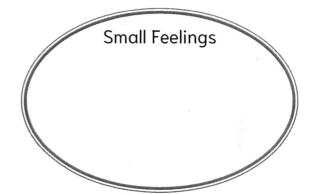
Small Feelings

Draw a picture of you having a BIG feeling AND a small feeling—at the same time!

Name: _____   **Date:** _____

Mindfulness Matters

Taking a deep breath or doing a yoga pose can help with your big feelings.

When your mind and body are calm, you can focus on what to do next.

Let's take a look at what you have learned about mindfulness.

Do you have a favorite yoga pose? Draw it here. You could also draw one you want to try.

Do you ever stop and take a deep breath? How does it feel? _____

_____

_____

_____

What is the best way you have learned to calm yourself down? _____

_____

_____

_____

Name: _____   **Date:** _____

In My Zones

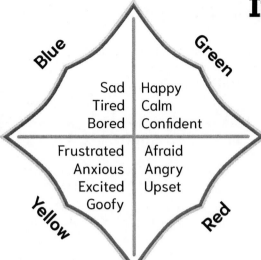

Your feelings change all the time. You could wake up happy. You might feel grumpy by lunchtime and a little tired in the afternoon. By evening, you could be sad or even angry!

You could move from one Feeling Zone to the next in a day. Or even in an hour!

How do you feel in a day? Write your answer, and color it in to match.

How did you feel when you woke up this morning?

How do you feel when you're in class?

How do you feel in the afternoon?

How do you feel at night?

Name: _____   Date: _____

How do you disagree?

When we disagree, our feelings are going to come up.

Disagreeing with someone can bring up feelings of anger, sadness, and loneliness.

How do you usually act in a disagreement? Color the ones that sound like you.

Yell or shout

Cry

Laugh

Get quiet

Walk away

Get help from an adult

Kick or hit

Take turns

Say you're sorry

Name: _____ **Date:** _____

What's the deal with how I feel?

For each situation, color what feelings you might have. You can use more than one color in a box.

Red = Angry	Orange = Afraid	Yellow = Worried	Green = Happy	Blue = Sad	Purple = Calm

A big storm is coming.	Someone teases me.	I hear my favorite song.
I lose a game.	I'm playing with my pet.	I dropped my ice cream.
I have to say I'm sorry.	My favorite shirt is ruined.	I have a cold.

Name: _____   Date: _____

Being kind is cool.

By now you know—we all have feelings!

Knowing that we are all so alike, can you feel a little kinder toward others?

Spreading kindness helps us all feel happier.

Let's practice some kindness today!

What is something kind you have done for someone else lately? _____

_____

_____

_____

What is something kind someone has done for you lately? _____

_____

_____

_____

Draw a picture of something kind you can do for someone else today.